A TASTE OF MERSEYSIDE

by
Master Chef Tom Bridge

Foreword by BBC Radio Merseyside's Tony Snell

95.8 FM BBC RADIO MERSEYSIDE

B B C RADIO MERSEYSIDE

in association with

Avid Publications,
Garth Boulevard,
Bebington,
Wirral,
Merseyside. CH63 5LS
Telephone / Fax: (44) 0151 645 2047
e-mail info @ AvidPublications.co.uk
website http//www.AvidPublications

A TASTE OF MERSEYSIDE

by Masterchef Tom Bridge
ISBN 1 902964 2 3 3
© BBC Radio Merseyside 2001

Editing, Typeset and cover design by William David Roberts MA © **2001 Avid Publications.**

Front Cover: Tom Bridge and Tony Snell in the BBC Radio Merseyside Kitchen.
Photography by M.G Photography, Woolton, Liverpool, L25 8SW.
0151 428 8099 / 724 2972

The Author - Tom Bridge.
Aged 4.
Who would have thought he would
turn out to be a cook?

A complete listing with prices of many other
books and videos from Avid Publications is at
the back of this book.
To Order Books or Videos Direct Contact:-
Avid Publications,
Garth Boulevard,
Hr. Bebington, Wirral,
Merseyside UK.
CH63 5LS.
Tel / Fax 0151 645 2047
Look at the books and videos via the internet
on
http://www.avidpublications.co.uk
e-mail info@AvidPublications.co.uk

Foreword

by BBC Radio Merseyside's Tony Snell

If there were a political correctness law for food Tom Bridge would have been behind bars long ago! He is the only chef I know (in fact he *is* the only chef I know) who could put bacon, cheese and tomato between two slices of malt loaf and make it taste absolutely delicious. We live in troubled times when it comes to food and what was good for you yesterday is a big 'no no' today! I don't know whether I'm a full fat, half fat or semi skimmed man from one day to the next.

Tom Bridge first came to my attention when I read an article he'd written about that great Liverpool delicacy, Scouse. How can a big 'Woolyback' like Tom Bridge know about the intricacies and delicate nature of making this fine dish? Well that's easy, his auntie Doreen from Bootle gave him her secret recipe! We made contact soon after and from that first appearance on my show Tom was an instant hit with the listeners. His down to earth nature and his fantastic advice like: "Oh forget the low fat spread luv, shove in some dripping" had them remembering a bygone age of food; days when putting a lining on your stomach before a night on the tiles wasn't considered a bad thing and corned beef hash was the staple diet of millions.

Over the years Tom has prepared food for Royalty and even the Queen, well not Her Majesty but Queen at the Live Aid concert when he was the head chef looking after food for the performers. His style of presentation with his ginormous blue plates and his fluorescent yellow knives and forks make tasting his creations an event. In fact he is the main reason for my extra stone since we met, as I am chief taster every Wednesday. So let Tom remind you of some of those old Merseyside recipes 'that yer mother used to make'.

Bon Appetit! (which is French for "get it down ya lad!")

Snell x

Author's Introduction

*H*aving spent most of my working life in kitchens around Britain, I had really never considered the power behind the food produced in the North of England. Until now that is...

During my visits to Merseyside, Cheshire and the surrounding areas I gradually came to realise that some of the best fare was right on my own doorstep! But what a well-kept secret it is! The BBC Radio Merseyside Cookbook contains a selection of mouth-watering recipes from the Home & Hearth of the North with seven chapters of easy-to-follow recipes.

Join me in the forthcoming pages for a springtime picnic in the heart of our beautiful Northern countryside. Butties and barbecues taste that much better when you're relaxing with friends and family on a beach or overlooking a lush green meadow.

Thanks to all the friends I've made since coming into Snelly's show every Wednesday morning on BBC Radio Merseyside I really believe we've come up with a range of recipes that will make the South gasp with envy!

What other region could produce such a range of food for every occasion? Liverpool Bun Loaf, Toad in the Hole, Scouse, Everton Toffee, Wet Nelly ...to name just a few. AND we've come up with recipes suitable for EVERY time of year -

Autumn brings out some of the finest fish from around the Lancashire and North Wales coast with enough sea bass, oysters, sole, mullet, sea bream, brill and salmon to make the continentals cringe with envy !

Such traditional recipes from Merseyside (and a bit beyond !) will help to relive the true heritage of yesteryear so that you can try for yourself in your own kitchen the recipes of that golden era when food really was at its best.

We return to the days when there was no need to advertise organic produce because the eggs came from a real chicken not an ever-ready hen. When flour was milled over and over again to make it super-fine and the milk came from the cows that chewed the lush grass from the Northern Moors around North West Lancashire, Cheshire and Merseyside.

Such were the eating traditions of a friendly and hardworking people, whose love of food can now be spread to every family table in the country. Yes even down South!

You too can relive the times when every family warmed the pot to make the tea, when the bread and cakes were always warm and pots and kettles were suspended above the hearth. A time when farmhouse kitchens had hams hanging from the ceiling and the smell of new bread lay heavy in the air...

Such traditions live on today despite the proliferation of fast-food restaurants and convenience food. The pie recipes in this book showcase beautifully the talents of generations of Northern families... such as the marble like colours of Four Layer Cheese, Venison pastie with pastry that melts in your mouth and Scouse (again!) to warm the cockles on a windy Liverpool winter's night...

Winter comes very quickly around Merseyside and my Winter Warmers and other recipes like Oxtail Soup with Fresh Tarragon Dumplings, Roast Sirloin of Beef with Herb Stuffing will certainly keep out the cold.

Don't believe what the detractors would have you believe! There is no other region in England that is so picturesque as the North, as anyone who has looked over the Wirral Way when the snow is lightly covering the treetops will tell you. In fact it was in Hoylake many years ago that I came up with my own favourite Christmas feast - the so-called 'Posh Nosh' recipes you'll find in section six, that starts with a light-hearted breakfast of Champagne Fruit Salad and Smoked Salmon with Scrambled Eggs. Then there is a fantasia of food that is typical of our love for the Festive season like my Christmas Pie, Venison Roast, Plum Pudding and Trifle. Rediscover tastes from mother's table of Duckling in Orange, Brandy sauce, Breast of Quail filled with Duck Liver, Port and Mushrooms and Roast Turkey with Lemon and Orange Stuffing plus a great deal more...All feasts fit for a Northern King and Queen !

The final section puts the spotlight on our jams and preserves, homemade strawberry jam, cranberry jelly, piccalilli, and mouth-watering beetroot and rhubarb chutney... really designed to sharpen your taste buds.

I'm delighted that you have chosen my book above the many other cookery books that adorn our bookstands and I sincerely hope you'll enjoy the recipes!

A TASTE OF MERSEYSIDE

Cooking with traditional Merseyside recipes

by

Tom Bridge - Master chef

ACKNOWLEDGEMENTS

The author Tom Bridge would like to thank:

Everyone at BBC Radio Merseyside especially Mick Ord and Tony Snell for having the faith in my work. Norman, Brian and Denis Olverson, all my girlfriends, Yo Yo, Ruth, Brenda, and the beautiful Amanda Jayne at Red Velvet Beetroot in Scarisbrick, Oliver Kay for supplying me with all the Fresh Fruit & vegetables required to test my recipes.
The meat men in my life - Scott's of Ormskirk, England's at Pemberton, near Wigan and good Ole Jack Morris at Farnworth near Bolton one of the top Butchers in the North.... thank you. Everyone at Asda Stores Walton, Freda Conroy and my chef buddy Mark Finney at Everton FC. My publisher David Roberts at Avid, who's helped make my job quite easy. Dave Hinds, because he's mentioned in every one of my cookery books. The whole of the Melia family, Aunty Do, Jim Owens and everyone in the Radio BBC Merseyside region for all their help and support to produce this wonderful cookbook. There is a list of addresses at the back of the book, giving you names and information on what you can buy and where... handy ain't it?

This book is dedicated to the memory of Joan and Jim Fitzpatrick

A TASTE OF MERSEYSIDE

SOME USEFUL INFORMATION.

All conversions are approximate.
(Use either system, but do not mix)

Weight

Imperial	Metric
¼ oz	7-8g
½ oz	15g
¾ oz	20g
1oz	25g
2 oz	50g
3oz	75g
4oz(¼lb)	100g
5oz	140g
6oz	170g
7oz	200g
8oz(½lb)	225g
9oz	255g
10oz	285g
11oz	310g
12oz(¾lb)	340g
13oz	370g
14oz	400g
15oz	425g
16oz(1lb)	450g
2lb	900g
3lb	1.35kg
4lb	1.8kg
5lb	2.3kg
10lb	4.5kg

Liquid measures

Imperial	ml	fl
1¾ pints	1000(1L)	35
1 pint	570	20
¾ pint	425	15
½ pint	290	10
¼ pint	150	5
2 scant teaspoons	28	2
1 teaspoon	5	

Length

Imperial	Metric
½ inch	1centimetre (cm)
1 inch	2.5 cm
2 inch	5.0 cm
6 inch	15 cm
12 inch	30 cm

Oven temperatures

°C	°F	Gas Mark
70	150	¼
80	175	¼
100	200	½
110	225	½
130	250	1
140	275	1
150	300	2
170	325	3
180	350	4
190	375	5
200	400	6
220	425	7
230	450	8
240	475	8
250	500	9
270	525	9
290	550	9

Serving quantities

Unless stated otherwise all recipes in this book are for 4 servings.

THE MOST REQUESTED BBC RADIO MERSEYSIDE RECIPES

WET NELLIE

This is a very old Liverpool recipe and I would love to know who Nellie was. Does anyone know? Especially for Freda at Asda stores at Walton, Liverpool.

Ingredients:

450g / 1 lb Shortcrust Pastry
225g / 8 oz trifle sponges, broken into fine crumbs
110 / 4 oz raisins
grated rind and juice of a lemon
4 tablespoon milk
110g / 4 oz golden syrup
milk and caster sugar to glaze

Method:

Set the oven at Gas mark 5 190c / 375f

Line a 18cm / 7 inch sandwich tin with the pastry.
Mix together the sponge crumbs, raisins, lemon rind, lemon juice, milk and syrup.
Place the mixture in the pastry case. Roll out the remaining pastry and cover the filling.
Seal and trim the edges. Brush with a little milk and sprinkle with caster sugar. Bake in a pre-heated oven for 30 to 40 minutes.

EVERTON TOFFEE

My Auntie Doreen gave me this recipe. Toffee is very easy to make if you can remember the following levels of sugar boiling:-
Mark Finney you'll have to make this for the Team !

Smooth: is reached when the sugar thermometer registers 215 - 220f
This degree is suitable for crystallising and making soft pastille goods.

Thread: 230-235f

Feather or blow: 240-245f, this is suitable for candying fruits and making fondants and creams

Ball or Pearl: 250-255f

Crack: 310-315f, this is the one required for the Everton Toffee and Everton Mints

Ingredients:

225g / 8 oz best butter
450g / 1 lb sugar (brown sugar for butterscotch)
225g / 8 oz golden syrup (treacle syrup for bonfire toffee)
6 drops of essence of lemon

Method:

Melt the butter in a heavy-duty saucepan, add the sugar and syrup and boil slowly for 3 minutes, until everything is blended. Then bring to the boil until the temp reaches 290 to 310f (crack stage) this should take about 20 minutes. just before the toffee is done add the essence of lemon. Butter and line a shallow baking tray, pour on the toffee, allow it to cool slightly then cut it into small squares and allow it to set.
For the Everton mint replace the essence of lemon with essence of mint using ten to twelve drops of mint.

BACON OLIVES

From the Fanny Calder School of Cookery, Liverpool 1904
This was a popular Breakfast dish in Liverpool.

Ingredients:

125g / 4 oz cold minced beef
50g / 2 oz breadcrumbs
1 teaspoon chopped parsley
25g / 1 oz chopped onion
1 teaspoon dried herbs
salt and pepper
a little egg
8 rashers of rindless middle cut bacon cut thin and halved
8 squares of fried bread

Method:

Gas 6 , 200c / 400f
Mix all the other ingredients together, to make a form of stuffing, except the bacon and fried bread.
Spread a tablespoon onto each slice of bacon and roll them up and put them onto a baking tray.
Bake for 15 minutes. Serve two bacon olives onto each slice of hot fried bread.

LOVELY LINDA McDERMOTT'S OLD FASHIONED LIVERPOOL BUN LOAF

Well what would BBC Radio Merseyside be without the lovely Linda McDermott! You can listen to her weekdays from 6.00am until Snelly appears at 8.30am.

Ingredients:

Make up 900g / 2 lb bread dough
6 oz butter
8 oz candied peel
8 oz raisins
teaspoon mixed spice
pinch of salt
1 tablespoon sugar

Method:

Set the oven Gas mark 6 , 200c / 400f

Melt the butter and work it into the bread dough, add the candied peel, raisins and spice, kneading it in with the salt and sugar.
Put the mixture into a buttered bread tin. Let it rise in a warm area covered with a warm tea towel for 40 minutes.
Then bake in the centre of the oven for 40 to 50 minutes.
Serve with fresh butter.

Serves: 4

EASTER SIMNEL CAKE

Easter would not be Easter without Simnel Cake; the 11 marzipan balls represent the apostles (Judas got the red card !) . They should be made into an egg shape, which represents spring and the rebirth.

Ingredients:

225g / 8 oz Plain flour
Pinch of salt
Pinch of baking powder
55g / 2 oz Rice flour
225g / 8 oz best butter
225g / 8 oz caster sugar
grated rind of 1 lemon
4 large (free range) egg's, separated
225g / 8 oz sultanas
110g / 4 oz glace cherries
110g / 4 oz raisins
110g / 4 oz currants
55g / 2 oz candied peel, chopped
340g / 12 oz white marzipan
1 egg, separated

Method:

Line a 25cm / 10 inch cake tin with a double layer of greaseproof paper.
Sift the flours, salt and baking powder into a bowl.
Cream the butter until soft and fluffy, add the sugar and lemon rind and whisk into the butter.
Beat in the egg yolks and whisk the egg whites until they are stiff.
Fold a little of the flour into the mixture, folding in the egg whites by degrees, add slowly the remaining flour, peel and fruits.
Pre-heat the oven gas 4 , 350f / 180c.
Roll out 1/3rd of the marzipan to fit the cake tin.
Put half the mixture into the cake tin top with the round of marzipan and then add the remaining mixture.
Wrap the cake tin in brown paper and then bake in the centre of the oven for 2 hours then reduce the heat to gas mark 2 300f / 150c for a further 20 minutes.
Allow the cake to cool. Roll out the remaining marzipan to the size of the top of the cake, egg white the top of the round and then shape the remaining marzipan into 11 small egg shapes and place them around the cake and egg white them also.
Tie a bright coloured ribbon around the side of the cake, sprinkle with icing sugar and it's ready for Easter Sunday

ENGLISH PARKIN

The battle between Lancashire & Yorkshire, still continues on the origin of this recipe, Graham & Rosie Wild whose families have lived in the Doncaster area, are convinced it really did come from that area. Maybe like the Yorkshire Treacle Tart and Mint Pasty, we should agree that no matter what area they come from they are still the best of British recipes.

Ingredients:

225g / 8 oz Plain flour
10ml / 2 teaspoon baking powder
pinch of salt
50g / 2 oz brown sugar
10ml / 2 teaspoon ground ginger
pinch of nutmeg
100g / 4 oz butter
225g / 8 oz black treacle
225g / 8 oz oatmeal
75ml / 2 fl oz milk
pinch of bicarbonate of soda

Method:

Pre-heat the oven to Gas Mark 4, 150c / 300f
Into a large bowl lightly mix the flour and baking powder, oatmeal, ginger, salt, sugar, nutmeg and bicarbonate of soda.
Melt the treacle and butter in a saucepan, add this to the dry ingredients, slowly adding the milk.
Line a bread baking tin with greaseproof paper and pour in the mixture.
Bake in the centre of the oven for 45 minutes.

MANX CAKE

This recipe I found in my copy of Warnes Model Cookery 1868 by Mary Jewry and I thought you might like to try it, it is very similar to Rice cake.
I have converted the recipe for the people of the Isle of Man who enjoy listening to Billy Butler, (you must be as mad as the rest of his fans.)

Ingredients:

25g / 1 oz butter
225g / 8 oz rice flour
225g / 8 oz granulated sugar
8 eggs
grated peel of ½ lemon

Method:

Pre-heat the oven to Gas 5, 375f / 190c.
Butter a 18cm / 7 inch sandwich cake tin.
Put the eggs in a blender and blend for 5 minutes or place them into a bowl, using a hand whisk blend for 10 minutes.
Sieve the rice flour into the eggs and blend, add the sugar and lemon rind and give the mixture a good stir.
Pour the mixture into the buttered cake tin, cover the top with a piece of greased , greaseproof paper and bake in the centre of the oven for 40 minutes.

From one giddy "KIPPER" to another

MRS MELIAS CORNED BEEF HASH
For Sophie, Daisy and our Tom

This is one of those recipes you would see in every cafe throughout Great Britain.

I remember a winter's day in Southport, a little cafe near the station. I ordered a cup of tea and all I could smell was fried onions. I asked the waitress what they were cooking and she said a corned beef hash for lunch, so I returned an hour later to enjoy a taste of tradition.

Ingredients:

450g / 1 lb tin of corned beef
25g / 1 oz beef dripping
1 large onion chopped roughly
600ml / 1 pint of beef stock, thicken with a little cornstarch
1 tablespoon mushroom ketchup
900g / 2 lb cooked and mashed potatoes (buttered & seasoned)
50g / 2 oz butter melted
75g /3 oz grated Cheddar cheese
freshly ground black pepper

Method:

Pre-heat the oven to Gas 4, 180c/350f.

Chop the corned beef into half inch cubes, place into a casserole dish, gently fry the onions in a little dripping then top the dish , sprinkle with mushroom ketchup, cover with beef stock.

Top with the mashed potato, melted butter and grated cheese, season with freshly milled black pepper.

Bake until Golden Brown for 20 to 25 minutes.

PETE VICKERS' PORK CUTLETS

Lancashire and Merseyside are still mad on pork. One of the most famous recipes from this area during the 18th century is Love in Disguise, which was calves heart filled with a pork forcemeat, coated in breadcrumbs and baked in the oven. This is quite a simple 19th century recipe that could possibly have been served during a hunt supper. Every choice cut is used in the making of pies, sausages, and hams. The alternative for this dish is to use veal cutlets should you not like using pork.

Ingredients:

50g / 2oz butter
4 x 250g / 9 oz Pork cutlets, trimmed
1 large onion sliced
2 apples, peeled, cored and sliced
25g / 1 oz butter
175g / 6 oz button mushrooms
1 tablespoon chopped coriander leaves
8 black peppercorns
1 tablespoon sesame seeds
2 large tomatoes, cut in half
salt & freshly milled black pepper
coriander leaves

Method:

Pre-heat the oven to Gas 2, 300f / 150c.
Melt the butter in a large frying pan and gently fry the cutlets for 5 minutes either side, remove the cutlets from the pan, place onto a dish. Keep them warm in the oven.
In the same frying pan, fry the onions and apple slices together, browning the apple slightly.
Place the apple and onions onto a serving dish, arrange the cutlets, placing them onto the onion and apple slices, and keep warm in the oven.
In the same frying pan melt the remaining butter and gently fry the mushrooms, coriander and peppercorns. Cook for 3 minutes then sprinkle the sesame seeds onto the mushrooms.
Place the mushroom, peppercorns and juices onto the cutlets, place the tomatoes around the edge of the cutlets and return to the oven for a further 5 minutes.
Season them well with salt and freshly milled black pepper, garnished with coriander leaves before serving.

FARMHOUSE GRILL

One of my favourite pubs in Liverpool is The Liffey on Renshaw Street
and they make an excellent Farmhouse Grill and Dublin Coddle.
For Bob Burns

Ingredients:

4 lamb cutlets, trimmed
4 pork sausages
4 x 175g / 6 oz rump steak
4 x 100g / 4 oz gammon steak
1 ring of black pudding cut into four, skin removed
2 lambs or pigs kidneys, cut into half
225g / 8 oz button mushrooms
2 large beef tomatoes
salt
freshly milled black pepper
fresh watercress for garnish
4 x rings of pineapple or 4 poached eggs

Method:

Season well with salt and freshly milled pepper all the meats, grill all the
meats until cooked approx 4 minutes either side.
Grill or fry the black pudding 3 minutes either side.
Place them onto a large serving dish and keep them hot in a warm oven.
Into a large frying pan add 2 tablespoons of cooking oil and gently fry the
mushrooms and tomatoes for 3 minutes.

Place them around the meats, garnish with some watercress, top the
gammon steaks with a fresh ring of pineapple or a poached egg.

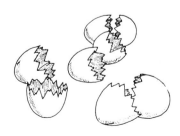

VICTORIAN POT ROAST BEEF

In days of old when Knights were bold and cookers hadn't been invented
They dug a hole in the middle of the ground and cooked to their hearts content.
This very ancient dish, is one of those that was copied by every cook and chef. Queen Victoria's chef Charles Elme Francatelli, claimed this to be his own recipe ! It was then called 'Braised Beef a la Polonaise aux Choux Rouges' 1862.
My version is a little more modern, but the flavours and method are still Victorian and Victorian Pot Roast is a regular feature on my dinner table.

Ingredients:

1.4 kg / 3 lb Topside of Beef
50g / 2 oz butter
20 shallots, peeled.
4 large potatoes, peeled and quartered
2 large carrots, peeled and cut into chunks
2 parsnips, peeled and cut into chunks
1 small turnip, peeled and chopped
1 sprig of fresh thyme
1 sprig of rosemary
salt & freshly milled black pepper
300ml / 10 fl oz beef stock
150ml / 5 fl oz of good quality red wine (not plonk)
2 tablespoons of cornflour blended with a little red wine

Method:

Quickly fry the topside of beef off in the butter, browning the beef well all over, then place to one side.
Fry the shallots, potatoes, carrot, parsnip & turnip in the butter and beef juice. Then place the beef, surrounded by the vegetables into a large deep casserole / pot. Add all the rest of the ingredients except the cornflour. Cover with a lid or cooking foil and place into the centre of the oven and cook for 2 hours. Half an hour before the meat is cooked remove the lid or foil , to allow the meat to brown a little more.
Carefully place the meat and vegetables onto a large serving dish, remove the thyme and rosemary sprigs and bring the stock juices to the boil and add the cornflour blended with a little wine. Cook and simmer for 4 minutes and pour around the vegetables. Serve garnished with fresh thyme.

ROGER'S RABBIT STEW WITH GUINNESS AND DUMPLINGS

Not one for Bugs Bunny, but this is Roger Phillips' favourite dish. Having beef stew without dumplings, is like having Roast Beef without Yorkshire pudding; I could just not face life ! Every town and village throughout the UK have their own versions and this is one of those really old village recipes from yester-year when Roger did not have a beard.

Ingredients:

900g / 2 lb Rabbit, fat and gristle removed & diced
50g / 2 oz flour, well seasoned
50g / 2 oz beef dripping
2 onions, peeled and sliced
600ml / 20 fl oz beef stock
salt
freshly milled black pepper
150ml / 5 fl oz Guinness
2 large potatoes, peeled and diced
1 large carrot, peeled and diced
175g / 6 oz button mushrooms, sliced
175g / 6 oz peas
(For Dumplings see oxtail soup... page 77)

Method:

Toss the rabbit in the seasoned flour, heat the dripping in a large saucepan and fry the rabbit
and onions for 5 minutes, add the beef stock and stout, seasoning well with salt and freshly milled black pepper.
Bring the contents to the boil and remove any excess scum floating on the surface. Add the rest of the ingredients except the dumplings. Stewing slowly for 2 hours.
Add the dumplings and cook for a further 30 minutes. Serve this with a glass of cider.

NORM'S PAN FRIED LAMBS LIVER, ONIONS AND BACON

My second father Norman Olverson Senior lives in Spain for seventy five percent of the year, because that's where the sun is, but when he comes home he loves nowt better than this.
Lambs liver is good, but calves liver is even better.

Ingredients:

450g / 16 oz Lambs liver, thinly sliced
salt
freshly milled black pepper
25g / 1 oz plain flour
25g / 1 oz cooking oil
25g / 1 oz dripping
2 onions, sliced
225g / 8 oz smoked streaky bacon, rindless
150ml /5 fl oz good rich gravy

Method:

Season the liver with salt and freshly milled black pepper and dust with the flour.
Heat the oil and dripping and fry the liver quickly on both sides so that the liver remains pink.
Remove the liver from the pan and keep it warm.
Add the onions and bacon and cook for 4 minutes , add the gravy and simmer for 5 minutes. Return the liver and the juices back to the pan and simmer for a further 5 minutes.
Arrange slices of the liver, onion and bacon onto individual warm plates, strain the sauce through a non-metallic sieve and pour around the liver.
Serve with new potatoes and button mushrooms.

Serves: 4

SCOUSE

I have relatives all over Liverpool and they have to be the friendliest, most humorous and warm people I have ever met. The Melia family eat Scouse while singing 'the Crystal Chandelier'! My father-in-law Jim Fitzpatrick who lived in Bootle gave this recipe to me.

The Dockers in Liverpool came home to this after a solid week's work, then it was off to the pub for a well-deserved pint.

Again the recipes vary all over the place for scouse, some just use silverside, some add peas, some add Swede and many add red cabbage. This is about the best and tastiest recipe I have ever come across and my wife Jayne who is a Liverpool Belle swears this is the original recipe!

For Doreen Fitzpatrick, Park Lane, Bootle.

Ingredients:

900g / 2 lb Neck of lamb, fat removed and cut into cubes then soaked in 600ml / 1 pint beef stock overnight.

450g / 1 lb stewing steak, fat removed and cubed

50g / 2 oz beef dripping

3 large onions, peeled and sliced

900g / 2 lb potatoes, peeled and sliced

2 carrots, peeled and sliced

salt & thyme

freshly milled black pepper

Method:

Pre-heat the oven gas 3, 325f/ 170c.

Melt the beef dripping in a deep ovenproof casserole.

Remove the lamb from the beef stock and dry the meat in some paper kitchen towel.

Seal the lamb and beef quickly in the hot dripping, add the onions and cook for 6 minutes.

LOB all the ingredients into the casserole, adding the beef stock and just enough water to just cover the ingredients.

Place a lid onto the casserole or cover with cooking foil and cook in the centre of the oven for 4 hours until the Scouse is completely cooked and blended together.

For **BLIND SCOUSE** add an extra assortment of Vegetables 900g / 2lb omitting the meat.

Serves: 6

SCOUSE WITH NECK OF MUTTON

Taken from *Food in England* by Dorothy Hartley, 1954.
Lob = sheep; scouse = broth.

The neck portions are best made into lobscouse. Chop the joint neatly and, bending it, rub pepper and powdered thyme into the slits, and cover all with a dusting of seasoned flour.

Put a lump of fat at the bottom of an iron saucepan and fry the meat in this till lightly browned.

Meanwhile, cut up carrots, turnips, a little Swede or parsnip, some onions, or if you are using leeks they will be found to make a very delicate dish and should be sliced across and across, add a sprinkling of barley. (On no account put in either onions or leeks uncut, or they will stew to a soft, stringy lump, instead of permeating evenly.)

Add these to the meat and then cover the whole with a layer of sliced potatoes followed by a layer of whole potatoes. (The idea of the cut layer is that they will simmer down in the cooking to a creamy mass and thicken the gravy.)

Add a good sprinkling of mountain herbs and fill up just to the level of the whole potatoes. (Note. The whole potatoes should not cook in the broth, but in the steam above the water level.)

Put on the lid closely and simmer very gently without stirring, till the top potatoes are cooked through (by which time the smaller vegetables, lower and nearer the heat, will be done, and the meat just leaving the bone). This dish is best served direct from the pot. If it is taken out, lift the potatoes and arrange them round the dish, and put the meat and vegetables in the centre. Circa 1850.

*The way we used to shop. Charlesworth's bakers used to be
in King Street Wallasey.
Photograph Courtesy Debbie Hughes whose Great
Grandparents used run the shop.*

IRISH SODA BREAD

Mrs Carol Lowry and husband Hubert from Newburgh, near Skem, enjoy this lightly buttered with lashings of Smoked Salmon.

Ingredients:

1 tablespoon bacon dripping or beef dripping
350g / 12 oz wheatmeal flour
350g / 12 oz plain white flour
1 teaspoon salt
50g / 2 oz lard, cut into small pieces
3 teaspoons bicarbonate of soda
2 tablespoons cream of tartar
1 tablespoon soft brown sugar
600ml / 1 pint buttermilk or half pint each of milk and single cream

Method:

Lightly grease a baking tray with the bacon dripping.
Pre-heat the oven gas 8, 450f / 230c.
Place the two flours into a bowl with the salt and blend together.
With your fingertips rub in the lard until the mixture resembles fine breadcrumbs.
Sprinkle in the bicarbonate of soda, cream of tartar and soft brown sugar, mix them all in together and add the buttermilk, using your hands blend and knead the dough very thoroughly.

Shape the dough into a ball and place onto the baking sheet.
Carefully press the ball down to form a disc shape, then cut into quarters, dust with the wheatmeal flour and bake in the oven for 30-35 minutes.
Allow the bread to cool for at least 15 minutes before serving.
Try this bread fried in bacon fat with white pudding and fried eggs at breakfast time.

B.B.B.B.   Yes it's that time again....BILLY BUTLER'S BARA BRITH

B.Bs listeners in Wales requested this recipe more than any other.
This speckled bread (Bara Brith) is a really nice bread to go with Caerphilly cheese for a real taste of North Wales. Originally served in the farmhouse and cottages during the Harvest festival , Easter and Yuletide log burning festival.
Also for Sydney in Oxton.

Ingredients:
25g / 1 oz butter
275g / 10 oz strong white flour
1 teaspoon of salt
25g / 1 oz lard
25g / 1 oz soft brown sugar
1 level teaspoon ground mixed spice
1 large egg, beaten
150ml / ¼ pint warm water
25g / 1 oz fresh yeast
225g / 8 oz currants
100g / 4 oz sultanas
50g / 2 oz chopped mixed peel

Method: Pre-heat the oven gas 4, 350f / 180c.
Lightly grease with the butter a 900g / 2 lb loaf tin or two 450g / 1 lb loaf tins.
Sieve the flour and salt into a large mixing bowl, add the lard and rub it into the flour, add the sugar and spice mixing again and make a well in the mixture. Blend the egg with the warm water and use two tablespoons to make a smooth paste with the yeast, then blend the paste back into the water.
Pour over the flour, mixing thoroughly and vigorously, then knead until it is like a smooth but elastic dough consistency. Add the currants, sultanas and mixed fruit, kneading them into the dough.
Roll it into a round but long shape to fit the loaf tin or divide to fit the two tins, should you be using two.
Place the tin onto a baking sheet and cover the loaf tin with greased cling film and put in a warm place for 2 hours. Remove the cling film and bake in the centre of the oven for 35 to 40 minutes until golden brown.
For a better crispier topping, add 1 tablespoon of apricot jam , coating the top of the bread and then sprinkle with poppy seeds at the 30 minute stage of the baking process.
Bake for the last ten minutes and serve with fresh salad and cheese.

LIVERPOOL CHRISTMAS LOAF

Liverpudlians have a unique sense of humour, I should know, I married one!
A Merseyside Christmas is always a family occasion with plenty of booze,
food and renditions of 'You'll Never Walk Alone' and 'In my Liverpool
Home'.
Kivers in Bebington helped out with this one.

Ingredients:

Ferment:-
75ml / 2 fl oz warm milk
15g / ½ oz fresh yeast
1 tablespoon sugar
50g / 2 oz strong white flour
1 egg beaten

Dough:-
100g / 4 oz lard
100g / 4 oz soft brown sugar
1 egg, beaten
1 tablespoon black treacle
225g / 8 oz strong white flour
1 teaspoon salt
1 teaspoon baking powder
1 teaspoon freshly grated nutmeg
1 tablespoon ground mixed spice
225g / 8 oz sultanas
100g / 4 oz currants
grated rind of 1 lemon and orange

Method:

Pre-heat the oven gas 6 , 400f / 200c
For the ferment mix all the ingredients thoroughly together in a warm
bowl, cover with cling film and place in a warm area for 25 minutes.
To make the dough, cream the lard, sugar and egg together, add the
treacle and all the rest of the ingredients. Mixing them thoroughly
together with the ferment mixture.
Place the dough into a buttered loaf tin, cover with cling film and place in
a warm area for 40 minutes. Remove the cling film and place into the
centre of the oven and bake for 50 to 60 minutes.
Serve with lashings of butter and fresh strawberry jam.

LAMB IN RED WINE (POSH SCOUSE)

I have seen this recipe completely ruined by over cooking and by using cheap wine. One should always use a good quality Burgundy when cooking with lamb to express the true character of this classical Merseyside dish. My recipe goes a stage further; I have now converted it into a healthy eating recipe.

Ingredients:

1.75 kg / 4lb Lamb diced
900g / 2 lb potatoes, diced
60ml / 4 tablespoon brandy
225g / 8 oz shallots, peeled
225g / 8 oz button mushrooms, trimmed
100g / 4 oz streaky bacon, cut into pieces
600ml / 1 pint chicken stock
45ml / 3 tablespoon seasoned flour
60ml / 4 tablespoon olive oil
salt
freshly milled black pepper
2 garlic cloves finely chopped
sprig of thyme
1 bay leaf
1 bottle of Red Burgundy wine
30ml / 2 tablespoon cornflour
60ml / 4 tablespoon finely chopped parsley

Method:

Cut and trim the lamb into serving pieces, making sure that all the excess fat and skin is removed.
In a large ovenproof casserole, heat the olive oil and sauté the pieces of potato, bacon, after two minutes add the shallots and mushrooms.
Cook for a further 3 minutes. Toss the pieces of lamb in the seasoned flour and sauté for 12 minutes, turning the lamb every 4 minutes.
Add garlic, thyme, parsley and bay leaf, season the casserole with salt and freshly ground black pepper.
Cover the casserole and place in the oven for 55 minutes.
Remove the lamb, bacon and vegetables from the casserole and keep them warm.
Skim off any excess fat from the lamb juices, pour in the warmed brandy and ignite, allowing it to burn out for at least two minutes.
Pour over the Burgundy wine, saving at least one glassful. Cook the wine until it is reduced by half the original quantity.
Add a little wine from the glass to the cornflour, making it into a paste, add the cornflour to the sauce, whisking it in.
Let the sauce cook for 4 minutes, then strain the sauce into a clean casserole, adding the lamb, bacon and vegetables. Let it simmer in the oven for a further 20 minutes.

Serves: 8

SECTION TWO

SUMMER PICNICS

This section is dedicated to the British Sandwich Association. To learn more contact them on 01235 821820 or e-mail: enq@sandwich.org.uk

This is my Butty section, ideal for the summer picnic, this should keep the missus's gob shut for an hour...

AMANDA'S RED VELVET PLOUGHMAN'S
*For the Amanda Jayne Aldred fanclub
or hotpants @ appleybridge.com*

Red Velvet is a beetroot grown in Scarisbrick, Lancashire and it is a natural product full of vitamin E, B and Iron, a blood purifier and a full source of calcium. It is washed, peeled and grated by hand and then ready for the table.
For more details take a look at the website @ www.redvelvet.co.uk.

Ingredients:

1 Greenhalgh's Fruit Loaf, cut and sliced lengthways into three layers
225g / 8 oz grated Lancashire Creamy Cheese
100g / 4 oz Red Velvet beetroot grated
1 bunch of fresh watercress
45 ml / 3 tablespoon apple puree
4 thin slices of York Ham
4 soft boiled eggs, mashed with butter and seasoned
30 ml / 2 tablespoon of mild lime pickle

Method:

Butter the fruit loaf and layer the first half with the cheese, red velvet and watercress. Top with the fruit loaf slice and then add the apple puree, ham, eggs topped with lime pickle.
Finish with the final slice of fruit loaf.

Place three to four cocktails sticks along the centre and slice between each cocktail stick and serve with a little salad and an Ice-cold glass of Cider

For the children use sweeter fillings like Peanut butter, chocolate paste, with cheese slices. Always put the meat or solid on for the first filling, this stops juices running through. Avoid watery sauces.
Serves: About 6 - Makes one big butty

A MEDITERRANEAN MOMENT

Yes this a sandwich full of sunshine from three very pretty girls, Bronagh Kennedy, Stephanie Woodworth and the talented Jessica Boulton.
This sandwich, which won the Greenhalgh's 2001 Sandwich Competition, and these girls from St. Antony's RC High School along with their teacher Mrs Gill Atkinson, devised this mouthwatering taste of summer.

Ingredients:

1 large white Roll (with Criss Cross Markings)
25g / 1 oz best butter
1 tablespoon of sun dried tomatoes and oil
1 tablespoon Parmesan cheese
100g / 4 oz chicken fillet
50g / 2 oz grated Mozzarella cheese
2 Italian Plum Tomatoes, sliced thinly
Continental salad
1 tablespoon Mayonnaise

Salad Dressing

1 tablespoon of Olive Oil, Lime, White wine vinegar and chopped Coriander

Method:

Cut the Roll lengthways and butter, lay out the bottom onto a dark serving plate.
Using a griddle pan cook the chicken fillet in the sun dried tomatoes and oil, when cooked allow it to cool slightly and slice thinly, sprinkle with Parmesan cheese and layer it on the bottom of the buttered roll.
Top with the rest of the ingredients, using the grated Mozzarella cheese, Italian Plum Tomatoes, sliced thinly, a generous coating of Continental salad, sprinkled with the Mayonnaise and Salad Dressing.
Place the top onto the sandwich and slice into halves and serve with some of the Continental Salad and a little more Salad Dressing

RON DAVIES' PERFECT LIVERPUDLIAN CLUB SANDWICH

If you want to know how a sandwich travels through Liverpool you have to ask Ron Davies.... and if everything comes to a standstill who's fault is it?

Ingredients:

2 thick large Greenhalgh's Ciabatta with Olives Bread
225g / 8 oz Chargrilled Smoked Chicken cut into thin slices
1 Yellow Pepper de-seeded and thinly sliced
30ml / 2 tablespoon. Parmesan
100g / 4 oz Rocket
100g / 4 oz Shredded Red Velvet Beetroot
225g / 8 oz Natural Cured British Crispy Bacon
100g / 4 oz Sun Blush Tomatoes

Balsamic Dressing
4 tablespoon Balsamic vinegar
8 tablespoon Extra Virgin Olive Oil
1 tablespoon English Mustard
8 Basil leaves ripped by hand
Salt
Freshly milled black Pepper

Method

Slice the Ciabatta lengthways, making the bread ready for a two-layer sandwich, butter lightly.
Then interlay the chicken, yellow peppers and Parmesan on the first layer, top with Ciabbatta, then add the rocket, Red Velvet, bacon, sun blush, sprinkled with the Balsamic Dressing.
This sandwich can be served hot or cold.

Serves: Makes four Club sandwiches

MERSEYSIDE SAVOURY MELTS

This recipe was first introduced in the second quarter of the 19th century, and certainly represents the quality of English cookery during this period. But today the kids love 'em.

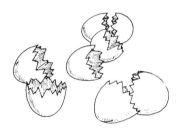

Ingredients:

4 slices medium or thick bread
50g / 2 oz soft butter
8 Anchovies
4 eggs
150ml / 5 fl oz double cream
50g / 2 oz Lancashire cheese, grated
Ground black pepper and salt

Method:

Toast the bread and butter well on both sides.
After washing and scraping the anchovies spread them between the two slices of toast.
Beat the yolks of the eggs with the cream and cheese and season well (a small pinch of cayenne may also be used).
Pour the liquid slowly into a saucepan and gently heat, taking care to only thicken but not to boil.
Remove the saucepan from the heat.
Pour liquid over the pieces of buttered toast, criss-crossing with anchovies and serve immediately.
For the more health conscious fromage frais may be used for a lighter texture.

DEEP FRIED BRIE WITH PLUM SAUCE in PITTA

Brie is also the name of a very small Irish woman and goes excellent with Beetroot ! You can also use any semi hard cheese like a Sage Derby or a Ridder from Norway or soft cheese such as Camembert, Limburger or a Kappeli from Finland.

Ingredients:

30ml / 2 tablespoon plain flour
450g / 1 lb Brie, cut into 6 wedges
1 egg, lightly beaten
50g / 2 oz fresh white breadcrumbs
corn oil, Plum sauce
6 rounds of Pitta Bread filled with Shredded Cos, Tomatoes and diced red onion

Method:

Sift the flour onto a plate and carefully coat the cheese all over, dip the wedges into the beaten egg and coat with breadcrumbs. Heat the oil in a deep frying pan or deep fat fryer to 180c /350f and deep fry the wedges for 2 minutes on either side until the breadcrumbs are golden brown. Drain on kitchen paper.
Warm the pitta bread and cut a pocket into each one, line with lettuce, tomato and onion, place a fried brie wedge into each pocket and serve hot with the Plum sauce.

Women making food! A Typical production line at Jacobs' Biscuits Aintree Factory. Photograph Courtesy Dolly Mitchell of Toxteth.

BIG JIM'S CHEESE & BACON MILLE FEUILLE

Alright you want to know who big Jim Winslip is, well J.W., as he is known down on the ranch, is head of the British Sandwich Association and he knows which side is bread is buttered.
Try any blue cheese for this recipe or a Ewes milk cheese like Roquefort. The cheese must really be strong enough to excel the bread, served with a Rioja wine or a tawny Port

Ingredients:

1 bloomer, cut lengthways X 4 and buttered
225g / 8 oz Blue Vinney cheese, crumbled
225g / 8 oz Buffalo cheese, finely chopped
225g / 8 oz Cheddar, grated
450g / 1 lb streaky bacon, grilled and chopped
2 tablespoons English Mustard
25g / 1 oz butter
freshly grated nutmeg
1 egg beaten with 1 tablespoon of port

Method:

Pre-heat the oven Gas 7, 220c / 425f.

Place the bottom of the bloomer on a greased baking sheet.
Put the cheese, bacon, butter, nutmeg and egg beaten with port into a bowl and cream. Spread the cheese mixture onto the base of the bloomer, moisten the edges with port and top with the second piece of buttered bread, repeat the process until everything is used up.
Then bake in the centre of the oven for 15 minutes until the bread is crisp and golden brown.
Remove from the oven, and allow it to cool slightly, slice and serve.

G.F. Stansfield's Butchers shop, 64 Robson Street, Anfield, in the 1930's.
Photograph Courtesy of the owners son, Mr C.G. Stansfield of Allerton.

BARA CARAWE

North Wales is populated with many ex - pat scousers who over the years have influenced and been influenced by Welsh cooking. This is one of my favourite breads and a good friend, David Hinds, gave this recipe to me when I used to visit him in Wales.
The bread must be warm and served with cold meat or cheese.

Ingredients:

600ml / 20 fl oz water
2 oz fresh yeast
350g / 12 oz strong white flour
350g / 12 oz wholemeal flour
225g / 8 oz oatmeal
1 teaspoon salt
1 tablespoon caraway seeds
50g/ 2 oz brown sugar

Method:

Pre-heat the oven Gas 6, 400f / 200c.

Put 4 tablespoons of warm water into a bowl and crumble in the yeast, leave the yeast for 5 minutes then blend in with the rest of the water.
Into a separate bowl add the flours, oatmeal, salt , caraway seeds and brown sugar, blending all the ingredients together. Add the yeast water to the dry ingredients. Mix and knead by hand for 10 minutes until the dough is developed, becomes slightly elastic. Leave in the bowl and cover with a warm damp cloth in a warm area for at least 1 hour.
Divide the dough into 2 equal pieces, place into two well greased loaf tins and bake in the centre of the oven for 35 minutes.

VINCENT'S ULTIMATE HEALTHY EATING SANDWICH

Every Monday lunchtime Vincent (I want a butty) Burke is with the bearded wonder Roger Phillips and when he finishes he enjoys nothing better than my butties...

Ingredients:

2 large Ciabatta sliced lengthways
8 slices of natural cured English bacon, grilled crispy
50g / 2 oz Spreadable, natural clear honey
100 / 4 oz York Ham thinly sliced
25g / 1 oz soft sugar free Cranberry Jelly
100g / 4 oz Sliced Turkey Breast meat
50g / 2 oz sliced red velvet beetroot
salt & freshly milled black pepper

Method:

Place the Ciabatta onto a large serving dish.
Place the slices of bacon with the honey for the first layer.
Add the slices of York ham followed by Cranberry Jelly. Season with salt and pepper then finally add the Turkey breast and beetroot, using the left over honey and jelly to top the turkey.
Place three toothpicks into the sandwich to divide to four servings and slice with a very sharp knife.
Serve with a light spring salad of endive, shredded celery and radish, topped with mustard cress.

Serves: 8

DAVE ROBERTS' SEA CROISSANTS

BBC Radio Merseyside's 'Maritime Man', Dave Roberts, tells tales of the sea with Snelly and enjoys just about anything with Tuna. Tuna is one of the top selling fish toppings in the sandwich market but to taste the best you must try this recipe using salmon.

Ingredients:

50g / 2 oz low fat margarine
2 shallots, sliced
6 basil leaves chopped
100g / 4 oz button mushrooms
100g / 4 oz smoked bacon, chopped
225g / 8 oz Tuna / Salmon fillet, skinned and boned
100g / 4 oz fresh water prawns
8 large croissants
tartar sauce, watercress

Method:

Warm oven Gas 4, 180c /350f

Melt the marg in a large frying pan
Cook the shallots, toss in the basil , mushrooms and bacon. Cook for 6 minutes, add the tuna / salmon, chopping it up as it cooks and blending with the other ingredients (about 7 minutes).
Cut the Croissants three-quarters of the way through and spread with tartar sauce and watercress.
Add the prawns to the tuna/salmon, cook for 2 minutes.
Place the mixture into each croissant.
Place onto a baking sheet and then into a warm oven for 3 minutes and serve.

THE BILLINGE STEAK BUTTY

For Eileen Watson and Hubby in Billinge, Wigan who always listen in on a Wednesday morning.. taaaaaaaa.

Ingredients:

2 French sticks sliced lengthways & buttered
8 x 75g / 3 oz Sirloin steaks, grilled until just cooked (pink)
8 slices of natural cured English bacon, grilled crispy
50g / 2 oz English Mustard
2 beef tomatoes, sliced
1 punnet of mustard cress, trimmed
50g / 2 oz sliced red velvet beetroot
salt & freshly milled black pepper

Method:

Discard the top of the first French stick, then place the bottom of the French stick onto a large serving dish.
Place 4 slices of Steak (hot) and bacon with the mustard for the first layer.
Top with the other bottom of the French stick, add the rest of the ingredients in order, top with the final buttered top, place cocktail sticks along it and serve.

Serves: 4 to 6

BOB 'THE BIRDMAN' HUGHES' POTTED CHICKEN & GAME

You need to get up early on Friday mornings to catch our Bob - BBC Radio Merseyside's answer to Bill Oddie !
Serve with hot buttered toast

Ingredients:

100g / 4 oz butter
450g / 1 lb cooked chicken meat, minced
100g / 4 oz cooked chicken livers, minced
1 teaspoon freshly grated ginger
freshly milled black pepper
2 tablespoon Rowan jelly (see page 116)
225g / 8 oz cooked venison roughly sliced
8 Orange slices
10 black olives, stoned
100g / 4 oz smoked duck breast

Method:

Beat the butter with the minced chicken, livers, ginger, freshly milled black pepper and Rowan jelly, blend thoroughly.
Add the cooked venison and interlay the mixture of smooth and rough game into small individual buttered pots or one large earthenware dish, top with slices of Orange and olives.
Cut the smoked duck breast meat into small diamond shapes and garnish around the edge of the game pots or dish.
Chill for 4 hours and serve with homemade toasted bread and a glass of Red wine.

TOM'S HOME-MADE BAGELS & SMOOTH CHICKEN PATE

Ingredients:

450g / 1 lb unbleached white bread flour
2 teaspoon salt
15g / 1 tablespoon fresh yeast
230 ml / $7\frac{1}{2}$ fl. oz of 50/50 milk and water
1 teaspoon sugar
25g / 1 oz melted butter
1 large egg, separated
flour for dusting
1 teaspoon olive oil
1 tablespoon warm honey
poppy seeds

Method:

Mix together the flour and salt in a large mixing bowl. Make a small well in the centre.

Crumble the yeast into a separate bowl and whisk in 100ml of warm milk/water mixture, add the sugar and let it stand for 15 minutes, Add the remaining milk mixture to the yeast and let it stand for a further 5 minutes.

Carefully pour the liquid into the well of flour, blending in with the butter, beaten egg white, working it all in with your fingers until it becomes a soft pliable dough, turn the dough out onto a floured working surface and cover with a warm damp tea towel for 10 minutes.

Knead the dough for 10 minutes, add any remaining flour. Then wash and clean the bowl, grease it lightly with a little olive oil. Place the dough back into the bowl, cover again with the warm damp tea towel and leave it in a warm area for 2 hours. Meanwhile make up my Chicken Pate ! (below)

Hit the dough like a boxer for 1 minute and divide the dough into a long, two inch thick rope, then divide it into 2 inch pieces, and roll each piece out to about six inches.

Taper the ends and place them well apart onto lightly greased baking sheets and leave them for 1 hour, they will double in size. Meanwhile pre-heat the oven to Gas 6, 400f / 200c.

Beat the egg yolk with the honey and lightly brush each bagel, sprinkle with poppy seeds and bake in the centre of the oven for 25 minutes Remove from the oven and let them cool.

CHICKEN LIVER PATÊ

Courtesy of Tabitha in Childwall - she may be posh but she knows her nosh!

900g mix for a 1 litre / $1\frac{3}{4}$ pint terrine

Ingredients:

100g/ 4 oz back pork fat, small dice
225g / 8 oz lean pork, minced
225g / 8 oz chicken, minced
225g / 8 oz chicken livers, minced
1 onion, finely chopped
1 teaspoon garlic powder
10 juniper berries, crushed
$\frac{1}{2}$ teaspoon allspice
$\frac{1}{2}$ teaspoon mace
4 tablespoon white wine
3 tablespoon brandy
salt fresh ground black pepper
2 eggs
285g / 10 oz smoked or streaky bacon

Method:

Preheat the oven gas 3 , 170c / 325f
Place all the ingredients into a food mixer and blend them thoroughly.
Line the terrine with streaky bacon.
Pour in the mixture, cover with slices of bacon.
Leave to mature for 6 hours
Cover the terrine with foil.
Place in a Bain Marie or a deep tray half filled with water and cook for 2 hours. The terrine must be left to mature after cooling for at least 2 days.
Serve with my homemade bagels, filled with cream cheese and this mouthwatering pate...yum.

CHICKEN, LIVER, BACON & ONION DOORSTEP

A doorstep in Merseyside is a thick chunk of bread about three inches deep, buttered and layered with your favourite nosh. Today this is posh nosh, happy cooking.

Ingredients:

8 smoked streaky bacon rashers, rindless and chopped
350g / 12 oz chicken liver, finely sliced
25g / 1 oz best dripping
450g / 1 lb King Edward potatoes, sliced
450g / 1 lb onions, chopped
salt
freshly milled black pepper
freshly chopped parsley
100g / 4 oz grated cheese
1 large tin loaf, cut into doorsteps and buttered
100g / 4 oz Lancashire cheese, grated

Method:

Melt the dripping in a large frying pan and cook the bacon and liver for 6 minutes. In a separate pan, fry the potatoes and onion and cook for a further 12 minutes.
Place the liver and bacon into a ovenproof casserole dish, top with the potatoes and onion. Add enough stock just to reach the potato based. Season and sprinkle with parsley and grated cheese.

Bake in the oven Gas mark 6, 200c, 400f for 25 minutes.

Allow the bake to cool for 15 minutes.

Serve this with doorsteps, thick cuts of bread, buttered, then layer the bake onto the bread... sprinkle with Lancashire cheese and return to the oven for 5 minutes.. is it any wonder I'm so slim...

ROGER LYONS' EGG, BACON AND SAUSAGE CRISS CROSS

Roger cannot resist this very tasty picnic bake after a 3 hour solid stint on Saturday mornings. It can be served hot or cold, and is very nice served with homemade Ginger Beer

Ingredients:

350g / 12 oz ready made shortcrust pastry
3 large hard-boiled eggs, shelled
8 rashers lean, rindless streaky bacon, grilled
225g / 8 oz sausage meat
1 egg beaten with 150ml / 5 fl oz milk
salt
freshly milled black pepper

Method:

Pre-heat the oven to Gas mark 6, 200c/400f.

Roll out 2/3rds of the pastry and line a buttered pie dish or deep plate with the pastry. Slice the eggs and chop the bacon and place those ingredients with small pieces of the sausage meat scattered around the pastry case. Pour over the egg and milk mixture.
Season the pie mixture contents.
Roll out the remaining pastry and cut into thin strips about $\frac{1}{2}$ inch and lay them across the pie to make a criss cross pattern across the pie, sealing well all around.
Bake in the centre of the oven for 10 minutes. Then reduce the heat to gas mark 4, 180c/350f for a further 25 minutes.

Serves 6.

DOUGIE'S SUMMER (ANYONE WHO HAD A HEART) SANDWICH

Douglas and Margaret Woods, live in Cleehill Road, Birkenhead. Dougie (a fun-ghi) loves mushrooms stuffed with Stilton. We got chatting and he sent me this recipe for his summer sandwich. You can still buy Ox heart from any good butchers, of which there are many on Merseyside.

Ingredients:

Ciabata Bread, sliced and buttered
75g/ 3 oz cooked Ox heart sliced
50g / 2 oz stuffing
75g / 3 oz York ham, thinly sliced
8 sliced peaches
50g / 2 oz grated Lancashire Cheese

Method:

Simply layer each ingredient onto the base of the bread and top with the ciabatta, slice and serve with a glass of good beer.

OPEN MOCK CRAB SANDWICHES

I first discovered this recipe by accident, while listening for the first time to the Beatles "Help" L.P. The music of the sixties, really does blend well with these very hip sandwiches. They are very colourful and you can use several extra ingredients should you wish to do so. Serves 6.

Ingredients:

6 thick slices of bread (crusts removed) or a large french stick cut lengthways then cut into 6 segments, then buttered
3 hard-boiled eggs, the yolk sieved & white chopped
25g / 1 oz softened butter
2 tablespoons of prepared English mustard
1 teaspoon anchovy essence
freshly milled black pepper
200g / 8 oz Wensleydale cheese
3 cooked chicken breasts, skinned and finely chopped
12 slices of each: tomato and cucumber

Method:

Reserve approx. the yolk and white from one egg.
Mix the remainder with the butter, mustard and anchovy essence, season well with the freshly ground black pepper.
Mix in the cheese and chicken and spread the mixture onto the bread. Interlay the egg yolk and white on the top of the spread, into alternate lines. Then line with tomato and then cucumber through the centre. Garnish with cress. Alternatively for the Posh Crab Sandwich use 450g / 1lb white and brown fresh crabmeat to emphasise the colours instead of the cheese and chicken. Add other ideas should you wish, like egg and cress, salmon and cucumber, tuna and mayonnaise, then garnish the edges around the sandwich with grated egg yolk and egg white.

PERCY'S PICNIC PIE

You'll know Percy from his many appearnces on Billy Maher and Alan Jackson's programmes...he is also a pie maniac.... and what a pie this is! Using layers of York ham, then raw eggs, the yolks kept whole, topped with cheese, then the process repeated; this
was the forerunner of the very first Ham & Egg Pie.
P.J. Proby was singing " Hold Me" and after eating a piece he split his pants.

Ingredients:

350g / 12 oz shortcrust pastry
450g / 16 oz York ham, thinly sliced
12 eggs
225g / 8 oz grated Cheddar cheese
salt
freshly milled black pepper
1 egg and a little milk whisked to coat the pastry lid

Method:

Pre-heat the oven to gas 5, 190c/375f.

Roll out two thirds of the pastry and grease and line a deep pie dish. Interlay the slices of ham, raw eggs and cheese, seasoning each layer with salt and freshly ground black pepper, ending with layers of York ham. Cover the pie with a pastry lid, seal and egg wash and bake in the oven for 25 minutes.

T.B's POTTED SMOKED TROUT

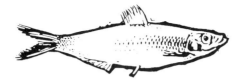

Quick and simple, this is one of those recipes that you can use trout, mackerel, crab, salmon or your favourite smoked fish. I first made this recipe when I was a " Bachelor Boy" on my "Summer Holiday" having a good time when Cliff Richard said... Tom,"Congratulations" and "The Minute You're Gone" I'm going to eat your Potted Smoked Trout. I replied just wait until "The Next Time" I make it.

Ingredients:

350g / 12 oz Smoked Trout fillets
freshly milled black pepper
2 tablespoons of English mustard
175g / 6 oz softened unsalted butter
juice of ½ lemon

Method:

Remove the skin from the trout fillets, place them into a blender or pound them in a bowl until they are smooth.
Add the mustard and softened butter, blending again until the whole mixture is very smooth add the lemon juice, blend. Serve chilled with fresh brown bread and butter. Pepper to taste.

Serves: 8-10

TRADITIONAL LEMONADE

There is no comparison between the bottled gassy lemonade you buy in the shop and the smell and taste of homemade lemonade, this is ideal for picnics and summer parties.

Ingredients:

2 litres boiling water
8 large lemons
200g / 8 oz granulated sugar

Method:

Wash and peel the lemons very finely, cut the lemon into half remove any white pith, from the strips of zest with a sharp knife. This prevents the lemonade tasting very bitter.
Into a large bowl put the zest and the lemons and their juice. Add the sugar and pour over 2 litres of boiling water, stir and cover with a clean dry towel and allow the lemonade to stand for 24 hours. Stir again then strain through a non-metallic sieve. Check for sweetness, add a little more sugar should you wish to do so. Should the lemonade be to strong, dilute it with some more water, or soda water.
Pour the lemonade into large serving jugs with plenty of ice. If you are taking the lemonade on a picnic, put ice into a large flask, pour in the lemonade and tighten the flask top.

FATHER O'MALLEY'S GINGER BEER

Father O'Mally is reputed to have made the best Ginger Beer on the North Docks. Legend has it that he tried to persuade the dockers to drink his produce instead of something a little stronger.... It is not recorded how successful this endeavour was, but his recipe lives on.

Ingredients:

450g / 1 lb sugar
Juice of 2 lemons
1 tablespoon of cream of tartar
75g / 3 oz fresh root ginger peeled and mashed
2 litres of boiling water
1 egg white

Method:

Into a very large bowl put the sugar, juice from the lemons, cream of tartar and the ginger. Pour over the boiling water and then stir in the egg white, which will clarify the ginger beer.
Let the liquid stand for 24 hours.
Stir the ginger beer, then strain through a fine non-metallic sieve. Bottle and allow the ginger beer to stand in a cool dark area for 4 days before drinking. This helps to improve the flavour.

BOTH THE LEMONADE AND THE GINGER BEER RECIPES SERVE ABOUT 14 PEOPLE

TOM'S LOVING CUP

There is plenty of romance in the North of England and champagne does flow in the heat of the summer, so why not try this soothing iced cold romantic drink.

Ingredients:

2 lemons, peeled and thinly sliced
4 teaspoons of sugar
6 fresh lemon balm leaves or spearmint leaves
600ml / 20 fl oz cold water
300ml / 10 fl oz Madeira wine
150ml / 5 fl oz Cognac
1 bottle of ice cold Champagne

Method:

Place all the ingredients except the Champagne into a large jug, stir and chill for 2 hours.
Just before serving, add the bottle of champagne and serve with fresh brandy snaps and strawberries.

Serves: approx. 14 drinks

STELL'S STRAWBERRY CREAM & CHAMPAGNE SURPRISE

Stell set up Radio Merseyside's 'A' team, and is also a dab hand at sweets.
This is one of the most delightful SURPRISE drinks that is so easy to make and yet, everyone will ask what is in it.
They will taste the strawberries and cream but not the Cointreau, which gives the unique flavour to this summer drink.

Ingredients:

225g / 8 oz fresh strawberries, washed and hulled
4 tablespoons of Strawberry Liqueur (Bols)
2 tablespoons Cointreau
lemon juice
150ml / 5 fl oz double cream
Crushed ice
1 bottle of Champagne
8 strawberries

Method:

Put the strawberries, liqueur, Cointreau and lemon juice into a blender and pulp it very fine. Add the cream and blend for 10 seconds.
Pour the strawberry and cream juice into a large jug. Top with crushed ice and strawberries, pour over the champagne. Chill for 1 hour and serve.

Serves: 8

CRISPY ROAST DUCK & BACON SALAD

Ingredients:

225g / 8 oz cold, Crispy Roast duck meat, skin removed
225g / 8 oz rindless streaky bacon, grilled until crispy
3 tablespoons Olive oil
1 tablespoon white wine vinegar
salt
freshly milled black pepper
50g / 2 oz cashew nuts
4 sticks celery, chopped
1 large dessert apple, cored and diced
1 large beetroot, cooked and diced
4 tablespoons mayonnaise
2 tablespoons of freshly chopped chives
1 crisp lettuce
2 oranges sliced into segments
2 beef tomatoes, sliced

Method:

Slice the cooked duck meat and bacon into bite size pieces and gently fry in the olive oil for a few minutes, remove from the heat and add the wine vinegar.
Season the duck and bacon with a little salt and plenty of freshly milled black pepper.
Place the duck and bacon into a large bowl toss in all the other ingredients except the lettuce, orange segments and tomato.
Onto a large oval plate decorate with the lettuce leaves to form a bowl shape, add the duck and bacon mixture into the centre of the lettuce and garnish with orange segments and slices of beef tomatoes.

MICK'S FAB SALAD

If it wasn't for Mick Ord this book would not have been written. This is the Boss' contribution... he says it's got a kick like a mule and is even better with hot chillies thrown in for good measure..

Ingredients:

450g / 1 lb cooked potatoes diced
1 tablespoon lime juice
8 Frankfurter sausages, cooked and chopped
225g / 8 oz cooked breast of chicken meat, chopped
2 large Red Velvet beetroots, cooked, peeled and diced
4 spring onions, peeled and chopped
150ml / 5 fl oz mayonnaise
freshly ground black pepper
Garnish: Crisp lettuce leaves, fresh mustard cress, 2 limes sliced and
2 beef tomatoes sliced

Method:

Carefully blend all the ingredients together and chill for 1 hour, place the mixture onto a bed of crisp lettuce leaves, garnished with mustard cress, sliced limes and beef tomatoes.

SIXTIES SALAD DAYS

Salads have been popular since the 1860's in the North. The same recipe is still popular today.... try it and you'll know why.
For Sandie in Nocturum

Ingredients:

1 small red cabbage shredded
1 large onion, peeled and sliced
2 carrots, peeled and grated
75g / 3 oz currants
1 tablespoon warmed honey
150ml / 5 fl oz thick mayonnaise
1 teaspoon curry paste
freshly milled black pepper
4 jacket potatoes (hot)
2 tablespoons of freshly snipped chives

Method:

Place the cabbage, onion, carrots and currants into a large salad bowl and toss them all together.
In a separate bowl, add the slightly warmed honey, mayonnaise, curry paste and freshly milled black pepper.
Put the vegetable ingredients in with the mayonnaise and blend.
Cut into the jacket potatoes scooping out a little of the potato, top with the salad and serve.

Before supermarkets.

Ashfield Farm Model Dairy used to be on Cherry Lane in Walton in the 1970's.

Photographs courtesy of Mr A.J. McCrane of West Derby

FOUR LAYER CHEESE PIE

The taste of my Three and Four-Layer Cheese Pie, which is my own invention, really is something else! The four colours of cheese, with a lining of spinach, fruit and onion between each layer, give a marble effect, when you slice into the pie.
I suggest Red Leicester, Lancashire, Double Gloucester and Yorkshire Wensleydale in that order for colour perfection, but you may use your favourites from all over Great Britain and Ireland.

Ingredients:

700g / 1.5 lb shortcrust pastry
50g / 2 oz butter
450g / 1 lb onions, chopped
350g / 12 oz spinach leaf, trimmed, blanched & chopped
175g / 6 oz of the following grated cheeses
Red Leicestershire, Lancashire, Double Gloucester and Wensleydale
8 tablespoons of apple puree
8 tablespoons of gooseberry puree
8 tablespoons of cranberry sauce
1 teaspoon of freshly grated nutmeg
Salt
Freshly milled black pepper
3 teaspoons Worcestershire sauce
1 egg mixed with 1 tablespoon of milk

Method:

Pre-heat the oven to gas mark 5, 190c/ 375f.
Roll out the pastry and use two-thirds of the pastry to line a deep 10in /25cm ring pie tin or loose- based cake tin, greased with a little butter
Fry the onion in a little butter 25g / 1 oz for 3 minutes. Add the spinach and cook for 2 minutes, season well with freshly milled black pepper and a little salt.
Lay a lining of the spinach and onion on the base of the pie, then top with the Red Leicester and apple puree.
Then add another lining of spinach and onion with the Double Gloucester and gooseberry puree on top.
Then a layer of spinach and onion topped with Lancashire . Repeat the process with the final cheese, the Wensleydale and cranberry, with a sprinkle of grated nutmeg and the Worcestershire sauce.
Use the remaining pastry to make the lid for the pie, sealing the edges, decorate the top with any left over pastry trimmings, and wash the top with the egg.
Bake in the centre of the oven for 45 to 50 minutes until golden brown.
Allow the pie to cool for at least 40 minutes.
Tom's tip: Serve at room temperature with a glass of chilled dry cider, with Baby Red Velvet Beetroot and light Mustard Mash.

Serves: 6 to 8.

SECTION THREE
BARBECUES

Barbecues reduce the tension that throwing a party produces; they are far more happy and casual affairs taking the weight off the shoulders of the hosts and allowing them to show off their ex 'boy scout' talents. On top of this, just like the picnic, there is the fresh air and healthy life that never fails to give your friends and guests a hearty appetite.
I always advise in this section do not use frozen or ready bought burgers, make your own, you then know what's in 'em!
Use a reputable English butcher, there are plenty around the North.

CAMELONANELEPHANTSBACKBURGER

Say it slowly and it's not so difficult; Camel - On- An-Elephants-Back-Burger; a whopping double lamb & beef burger with everything on it served with jacket potatoes with soured cream, roast corn on the cob with garlic bread a cooling glass of bitter.

Ingredients:

BURGERS
600g / 20 oz minced lamb
600g / 20 oz minced beef
3 large onions, finely chopped
100g / 4 oz fresh breadcrumbs
2 tablespoons Worcestershire sauce

FILLING
4 large burger buns
4 slices of Cheddar cheese
4 tablespoons of English mustard
4 tablespoons mayonnaise
shredded lettuce
2 beef tomatoes, sliced

Method:

Mix the minced lamb, with 1 chopped onion, 50g / 2 oz fresh breadcrumbs and 1 tablespoon of Worcestershire sauce.
Repeat the same process with the minced beef and shape into burgers.
Grill the burgers until they are cooked about 6 minutes on each side, fry the onions and toast the buns on the barbecue.
Place the bottom of each bun onto a serving plate, some cooked onion on the bottom of each bun, followed by the lamb burger, a
slice of cheese, with English mustard, beefburger, mayonnaise, shredded lettuce and tomato, topped with the top of the burger bun.

Serves: 4

ALAN JACKSON'S TOUCH OF CLASS

Alan's Merseyside Sports Special brings the sporting greats together, Liverpool, Everton and Tranmere to name but a few. Guaranteed to build up your team, just don't devour it too close to kick off.... A bit pricey, but then, like Gerard Houllier, we all have to splash out a bit now and again.

Ingredients:

900g / 2 lb fillet of beef
100g / 4 oz rough pate
2 tablespoons chopped chives
greased cooking foil
salt
freshly milled black pepper
50g /2 oz melted butter
150ml / 5 fl oz brandy

Method:

Slice the beef fillet down the centre, place the pate and chives along the fillet. Fold the fillet over to ensure the filling does not come out.
Place the fillet onto a large piece of cooking foil, season the steak well with salt and freshly milled black pepper.
Pour over the butter and half the brandy. Wrap and seal the beef fillet very securely in the foil. Cook over the barbecue for 12 minutes.
Remove the foil reserving the juices. Place onto the barbecue and grill until cooked, basting with the juices finally finishing the basting with the brandy.
Carefully slice and serve with garlic bread.

RON ROBY'S GLAZED GAMMON STEAKS WITH GOOSEBERRY SAUCE

Radio Merseyside's Rugby Union reporter is Yorkshire born and bred, and he brought the next two recipes over with him when he emigrated to Merseyside.
The finest ham in the world is York ham and there is no better way to serve it than with a rich gooseberry sauce.

Ingredients:

4 x 275g / 10 oz York Gammon Steaks, trimmed
4 tablespoons apricot jam
SAUCE
1kg / 2 lb gooseberries, topped and tailed
300ml / 10 fl oz sweet cider
250g / 8 oz brown sugar
25g / 1 oz ground allspice

Method:

Trim the gammon, making 1.5 cm / 1/2 inch cuts at 2.5 cm/ 1 inch intervals along the fatty edge, to stop the gammon curling.
Place the gammon steaks onto the barbecue grill and grill for 8 minutes either side, coating with the apricot jam for the last minute on either side.
Meanwhile put the gooseberries and cider into a saucepan and bring to the boil, simmer for 15 minutes then add the sugar and allspice and cook for a further 5 minutes.
Place the gammon steaks onto a serving dish, and generously coat each gammon steak with the gooseberry sauce.
Serve with Corn on the Cob and a light Potato salad.

BARNSLEY LAMB CHOPS IN FENNEL SAUCE

This sauce acts as a marinade and then a sauce, served with barbecued new potatoes and braised celery... these Barnsley chops melt in your mouth.

Ingredients:

4 x 275grms / 10 oz Barnsley chops, trimmed

MARINADE & SAUCE
150ml / 5 fl oz olive oil
2 teaspoons lemon juice
1 tablespoon white wine vinegar
1 large onion, chopped
1 teaspoon fennel seed, crushed
salt & freshly milled black pepper
2 tablespoons of port

Method:

Mix all the ingredients together in a bowl and leave the mixture to stand for 2 hours.
Add the chops, completely cover them with the marinade, chill for a further 2 hours.
Barbecue the chops for about 5 minutes either side.
Bring the sauce to the boil and reduce and simmer for 10 minutes. Strain through a non-metallic sieve and serve with the barbecued Barnsley chops.

LANKY LAMBURGERS

Rugby League's finest commentator, Ray French, came up with this one.......
go on... give it a **TRY** !

Ingredients:

8 spring onions, finely chopped
1 cooking apple, cored and finely chopped
2 tablespoons dripping
450g / 1 lb minced lamb
75g / 3 oz breadcrumbs
1 teaspoon crushed rosemary
1 tablespoon tomato ketchup
salt
freshly ground black pepper

Method:

Fry the spring onions and cooking apple in the dripping for 3 minutes.
remove from the heat allow to cool and blend thoroughly with all the remaining ingredients . Shape the lamb mixture into four burgers and grill on the barbecue for 7 minutes on each side.
Serve with a fresh mint salad and a glass of iced tea or an ice cold beer.

ALAN ROONEY'S PORK SPARE RIBS WITH GARLIC SAUCE

Another winner from a key member of our Rugby League Team

In most of the country homes, cottages and farmhouses they would have cured their own hams from their pigs and used the ribs for their dogs, but today they are more popular than ever for barbecues and with this garlic sauce, it will keep the devil or even your relatives at bay.

Ingredients:

2kg / 4 lb pork ribs cut into 7.5cm/3 inches in length

MARINADE
3 tablespoons, crushed garlic
120ml / 4 fl oz soy sauce
120ml / 4 fl oz sweet cider
4 tablespoons finely chopped spring onions
1 teaspoon crushed fennel seed
1 tablespoon tomato puree
2 tablespoons of clear honey
freshly milled black pepper
1 tablespoon of cornflour mixed with 2 tablespoons of dry sherry
5 tablespoons soured cream or yoghurt

Method:

Combine all the marinade ingredients except the cornflour paste and soured cream.
Add the ribs and mix well and let them marinade for 24 hours.
Remove the ribs from the marinade and place the ribs on the barbecue and cook for 5 minutes either side.
Place the marinade into a sauce pan, bring to the boil and simmer for 4 minutes, add the cornflour paste and soured cream, simmer for a further 3 minutes to make a thick creamy garlic sauce to serve with the ribs.

Try these ribs, with warm bread to dip into the sauce. Have a sprig of fresh parsley at hand to get rid of the smell of garlic from your breath after eating the ribs.
Simply wash the parsley in cold water and chew it for 2 minutes.

Serves: 8

PORK STEAKS WITH APPLE RINGS

The combination of flavours, from the mustard, bacon brown sugar and apple is astonishing.
Barbecues are really about experimentation, so add a few of your own flavours like a herb or pineapple ring instead of apple, garnish the steaks with mango or kiwi fruit. Enjoy yourself.......

Ingredients:

4 x 275g / 10 oz Pork steaks, edges trimmed
4 tablespoons English or Dijon mustard
4 apple rings
50g / 2 oz soft brown sugar
8 large rashers of rindless streaky smoked bacon
salt
freshly milled black pepper
sweet cider

Method:

Season the steaks well and barbecue them for 3 minutes either side.
Remove them and allow them to cool.
Coat them with mustard, top with a ring of apple sprinkle with some soft
brown sugar, wrap them in bacon and season again with salt and freshly
milled black pepper. Grill apple side down on the barbecue for 3 minutes
either side.
Sprinkle with a little sweet cider during the cooking process.

CHICKEN AND PINEAPPLE KEBABS

Try using fresh pineapple if you can, the tinned stuff I find too sweet and
does not taste anything like fresh pineapple.

Ingredients:

1kg / 2 lb Chicken meat, cut into small pieces
1 small pineapple, peeled and cubed
20 shallots, peeled and blanched
2 red peppers, de-seeded and cut into chunks
100g / 4 oz button mushrooms

Put all the ingredients into a marinade of:
1 tablespoon of lemon juice
1 tablespoon of walnut oil
1 tablespoon white wine vinegar
2 cloves garlic crushed
120ml / 4 fl oz soured cream
salt
freshly milled black pepper

Method:

Mix well all the chicken & ingredients with the marinade and chill for at
least 3 hours. Then remove all the food ingredients from the marinade and
alternate them onto the skewers. Grill them on the barbecue for 15
minutes, turning and basting with
the marinade every five minutes.
Serve the Chicken and Pineapple with a crisp tomato salad and an ice cold
bottle of white wine of your choice.

Serves: 6

CURRIED CHICKEN WINGS

Thanks to Eric & Barbie (Bar - B?) Coates of Bebington for this one...
they are big fans of Asian and Chinese food.

Quick, simple and to the point, this is the one dish to go first at
barbecues. You can also use duck, rabbit or venison meat for this recipe
should you wish to do so.

Ingredients:

24 chicken wings
3 cloves garlic crushed
1 large onion, peeled and chopped
3 tablespoons of mild curry paste
1 teaspoon crushed fennel seeds
150ml / 5 fl oz thick yoghurt
75g / 3 oz melted butter
1 tablespoon lemon juice
2 tablespoons sweet sherry
1 tablespoon Worcestershire sauce
freshly milled black pepper

Method:

Trim the chicken wings and place them to one side . In a large bowl place the other ingredients blending them thoroughly.
Add the chicken wings ensuring that they are completely covered. Let them stand for 3 hours, turning them every 15 minutes.
Place the wings onto the barbecue, grill and baste them for at least 4-5 minutes either side.
Heat the sauce on the barbecue for 6 minutes and serve with the chicken wings.

TOM'S SEAFOOD KEBABS

Ingredients:

450g / 1 lb uncooked King prawns, shell removed
26 scallops, shell removed
26 oysters, shell removed
4 tablespoons of oyster sauce
4 tablespoons of fresh lemon juice
50g / 2 oz clarified butter
3 tablespoons sesame oil
freshly milled black pepper

Method:

Place all the ingredients into large bowl, and allow them to marinade for 24 hours.
Place a king prawn, oyster and scallop onto each skewer.
Barbecue for 3-4 minutes, basting with the marinade , seasoning again with freshly milled black pepper before you serve them.
Place them onto a shallot or spring onion salad and serve with, chunks of garlic bread.

Serves: 8

SALMON STEAKS IN FOIL

Sheila from Ellesmere Port says her dad gave her this recipe in the 1940's - it still tastes just as good today as it ever did.
Salmon is a very versatile food and you can add almost any combination of your favourite herbs, butters and oils to the foil to create your own style of Salmon steak in foil.

Ingredients:

4 x 225g / 8 oz Salmon steaks,
buttered cooking foil
100g / 4 oz unsalted butter
4 tablespoons of lemon juice
4 tablespoons of lime juice
freshly milled black pepper
4 tablespoons freshly chopped parsley & chives
sourcream

Method:

Place the salmon steaks onto individual pieces of cooking foil, enough to completely seal, place 25g/ 1 oz of butter onto each salmon steak, dividing the rest of the ingredients also.
Wrap the steaks in the foil sealing them completely.
Place the fish in the fridge for 3 hours , bake the fish in the foil on the barbecue for 25 minutes until the salmon is tender.
Carefully open the foil and remove the salmon from the foil onto individual plates, reserving the juices in the foil.
Remove the centre bone and outer skin around the salmon steak.
Pour over the fish juices and serve with a sprig of fresh parsley, garnished with a little sour cream and freshly snipped chives.

Serves: 4

FRANKIE CONNER'S PRAWNS ON SKEWERS

Quick and easy, just like Frankie !

Ingredients:

900g / 2 lb uncooked Tiger Prawns, shell off
100g / 4 oz sesame oil
3 cloves garlic, crushed
2 tablespoons chopped parsley
150ml / 5 fl oz fresh lemon juice
freshly milled black pepper.

Method:

Wash and dry the prawns. Put all the ingredients in a flat baking tray, toss in the prawns, ensuring that they are completely covered.
Leave them to marinate for 3 hours.
Then put them onto skewers and barbecue them for 3 minutes either side, basting with the marinade.

CHEESY BAKED POTATOES with TUEBROOK SALAD

An almost anonymous recipe - I got a letter from a lady in Tuebrook but could not read her signature - this is dedicated to her.

Ingredients:

4 large baking potatoes
50g / 2 oz butter
50g / 2 oz grated cheese
4 tablespoons of soured cream
4 teaspoons of chives
salt & freshly milled black pepper
cooking foil

Method:

Scrub the potatoes in warm salt water, dry and prick them all over with a fork.
Parboil them for 10 minutes in hot salt water. Dry them cut a small wedge out of the centre.
Place on individual pieces of buttered cooking foil, divide the butter, cheese, cream and chives equally , seasoning the potatoes and double wrap them, making room for the butter, cheese, cream and chives to cook with the potato in the foil, on the top of the barbecue for 30 minutes.

Serves: 4

TUEBROOK SALAD

Simple and to the point, this is a mixture of vegetables and salad from the soil and farms around Merseyside.

Ingredients:

175g / 6 oz shredded white cabbage
75g / 3 oz chopped celery
75g / 3 oz grated carrot
1 bunch of spring onions, cleaned, ends removed and snipped
2 leeks, cleaned, using the white end only, chopped
3 chopped tomatoes
1 apple, cored, peeled and diced
4 tablespoons of mayonnaise
1 tablespoon freshly chopped basil
salt
freshly milled pepper
2 sprigs of fresh basil

Method:

Simply toss all the ingredients into a large salad bowl, season with salt and freshly milled black pepper and chill for 1 hour .
Add a little chopped basil with a fresh sprig of basil to garnish.

Serves: 6

BARBECUED BEANS

There are two main vegetables attached to barbecues, they are the potato, and corn on the cob buttered and wrapped in foil or cooked in its skin. But there cannot be a barby without beans, proper beans.

Ingredients:

25g / 1 oz butter
1 large onion
100g / 4 oz York ham diced
1 teaspoon hickory smoked sauce
½ teaspoon crushed fennel seeds
1 tablespoon American mustard
1 tablespoon Worcestershire sauce
425g / 15 oz beans in tomato sauce

Method:

Heat the butter in a large saucepan and fry the onions and ham for 5 minute. Add all the rest of the ingredients and simmer for 15 to 20 minutes on the barbecue. Check the seasoning and add a little salt if required and freshly milled black pepper.

TOM'S VEG ON SKEWERS

Ingredients:

450g / 1 lb Aubergines
450g / 1 lb green and yellow courgettes
1 red pepper
1 yellow pepper
450g / 1 lb red onions
1 teaspoon of crushed garlic
120ml / 4 fl oz olive oil
sea salt and freshly ground black pepper
1 teaspoon of oregano
1 teaspoon of chopped basil

Method :

Cut the aubergines into 1 to 2 inch cubes and soak in salt water for 20 minutes. Slice the rest of the vegetable into thick chunks and Interlay them onto wooden or metal skewers.
Coat with the garlic and olive oil, herbs and bbq for 6 minutes all round.

APPLES IN THE FOIL

This makes a really nice accompaniment to Pork or Duck or can also be used as a dessert for the barbecue.

Ingredients:

4 Dessert Apples, peeled and cored
50g / 2 oz melted butter
1 teaspoon crushed cloves
1 teaspoon cinnamon
4 tablespoons of sultanas
4 large pieces of buttered cooking foil

Method:

Place each apple into the centre of a piece of buttered cooking foil.
Put the butter, cloves, cinnamon and sultanas into a bowl and mix them together.
Pour a little of the sauce mixture over each apple. Seal them very tightly and place them on the top of the barbecue for at least 20-25 minutes until they are cooked.

AUTUMN

Autumn brings about some of the finest fish from around the Northwest of England, Sea Bream, Brill and Crabs with a catch of Oysters, Sole, Grey Mullet, Kippers and every type of seafood. Fleetwood is just a stones throw from here and I am sure these recipes will bring home, the assortment of fish produce we have in the Northwest.

FRESH SEA BASS STUFFED WITH VEGETABLES AND GINGER WITH A SPICY WHITE WINE SAUCE

This one might look a bit daunting - but well worth the effort if you take the time.

Ingredients:

THE STUFFING
50g / 2 oz of the following in Julienne Carrot, Leek & Celeriac
50g / 2 oz Mange Tout
2g / ½ oz Julienne fresh ginger
150ml / ¼ pint White wine
150ml / ¼ pint Creme Fraiche or Double Cream
salt
Freshly milled black pepper

Method:

Blanch the ginger for five minutes in boiling water.
Cook the julienne of carrot, leek, celeriac and Mange tout in the white wine.
When reduced and nearly cooked, add the ginger and cream, reduce again until the stuffing is thick , season & cool.

THE SEA BASS
8 X 100g / 4 oz sized medallions (filleted, skin & bones removed)
With a very sharp knife, cut a pocket into the medallion and stuff with the julienne of vegetables.

THE SAUCE
25g / 1 oz butter
4 shallots, peeled & chopped
10 cardamom pods
2 star anise
1 tablespoon Coriander seeds, crushed
Trimmings from the ginger
Black pepper
300ml / ½ pint of white wine
300ml / ½ pint fish stock
seasoning
300ml / ½ pint double cream or fromage frais
juice of 1 lemon

Cook the shallots off in the butter for 4 minutes, add the spices and cook
for a further 3 minutes.
Add the wine and fish stock, reduce by half, add the cream, and reduce
again by half.
Season well with salt and freshly milled black pepper, finish with
the lemon juice.
Pour the sauce over the medallions and garnish with fresh slices of lemon
and shredded leek & carrot.

ANDY BALL'S OYSTERS

Teamed up with Linda McDermott on
'Morning Merseyside', one of our Andy's
favourites is this classy yet traditional
dish.
Fit for a Toff !

Ingredients:

12 Oysters
50g / 2 oz best butter
50g / 2 oz plain flour
300ml / 10 fl oz dry white wine
2 shallots finely chopped
1 tablespoon finely chopped parsley
1 teaspoon anchovy essence
salt & freshly milled black pepper
175g / 6 oz white crabmeat
75g / 3 oz creamy Wensleydale cheese
75g / 3 oz Stilton cheese
125g / 4 oz Smoked salmon
175g / 6 oz fresh breadcrumbs
1 small jar of caviar
1 lemon very thinly sliced

Method:

Into a large Sauté pan poach the oysters in their own juice for 4 minutes.
Strain the juice into another saucepan.

Melt the butter in a saucepan and add the flour, cook for 2 minutes, blending all the time.

Add the white wine and shallots, bring to the boil and add the oyster juice.

Let it reduce by one third, about 1 hour.

Add the parsley, anchovy essence, seasoning well and cook for a further 15 minutes. Remove the pan from the heat and carefully blend in the oysters and crabmeat.

Spoon the mixture into individual ramekins, sprinkle with both cheeses, with a little smoked salmon, topped with breadcrumbs.

Bake in the oven for 12 minutes.

Serve with toasted garlic bread and finally top with a little Caviar and a piece of lemon before serving.

BILLY BUTLER'S FISH CASSEROLE

I have friends from every corner of Great Britain who always enjoy visiting this part of the country not just for their favourite beer but also for the day trips to Cavern Walks, The Albert Dock and my favourite pub the Liffey, which is very well known for this Fish Casserole. It really belongs to Sgt. Billy Butler, but I poached it 'cause it's my favourite.

Ingredients:

450g / 1 lb Brill fillets, skinned and chopped
450g / 1 lb Hake fillets, skinned and chopped
75g / 3 oz Plain, seasoned flour
salt
freshly milled black pepper
75g / 3 oz best butter
4 shallots, skinned and finely chopped
1 carrot, peeled and diced
1 leek, washed, and finely chopped
300ml / $\frac{1}{2}$ pint of fish stock
300ml / $\frac{1}{2}$ pint of medium white wine
2 teaspoon anchovy essence
1 tablespoon tarragon vinegar
chopped fresh parsley

Method:

Coat the fish in 25g/ 1 oz of the seasoned flour. Melt the butter in a flameproof casserole and add the fish, onion, carrot and leeks cooking gently for 10 minutes.

Sprinkle with the remaining flour, stirring for 2 minutes.

Slowly add the fish stock and wine, anchovy essence and tarragon vinegar.

Bring to the boil and simmer for 35 minutes on a low heat or bake in the oven for 30 minutes at Gas mark 4, 350f/180c.

Sprinkle with freshly chopped parsley and serve with warm crusty brown bread and a summer salad.

JIMMY MAC'S JACKET SPUD WITH SOLE

Made for the darkness of the Witching hour, when they were called Soles in their Coffins, during the Victorian autumn nights, when Jimmy MacCracken would prowl around Liverpool shining the top of his head in everyone's eyes...

Ingredients:

6 large baked potatoes
salt & freshly milled black pepper
12 small fillets of sole 100g / 4 oz
4 shallots, finely chopped
150ml /5 fl oz red wine
75g / 3 oz butter
100g / 4 oz button mushrooms, sliced
50g / 2 oz seasoned plain flour, sifted
300ml / ½ pint of warm milk
2 tablespoon double cream
175g / 6 oz fresh water prawns
1 sprig of fresh fennel

Method:

Pre-heat the oven to Gas mark 6, 200c/400f

Coat each fillet with a little wine, season them well and roll them up, skinned side inwards, holding them together with a small wooden skewer.
Poach them in a large frying pan for about 4 minutes in the red wine.
Carefully remove the fish from the pan, reserving the liquor.
In another saucepan add 50g / 1 oz butter, cook the mushroom and shallots for 2 minutes then add the seasoned flour. Slowly add the red wine stock and half the milk.
Simmer for 4 minutes , re-adjusting the seasoning. Remove the sauce from the heat. Blend in the double cream
Cut out a small slice from the Jacket potatoes, then using a tablespoon, carefully scoop out the centres and use the pulp with a little butter and milk to make a mashed potato.
Place the potato shells on a greased baking sheet . Remove the skewers from the fillets of sole. Put two sole fillets into each potato with some prawns and a little red wine sauce, pipe on the mashed potato and bake them for 8 minutes.
Serve them with the red wine sauce garnished with prawns and a sprig of fresh fennel.

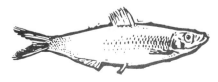

NORMAN THOMAS' GREY MULLET

This recipe is now served in a great deal of Chinese and Japanese restaurants around Great Britain; it is originally a West Derby 18th century recipe. With the addition of ginger and lemon grass it really does have a Chinese flavour to the recipes, but I do feel that little N.T. brought the recipe from London's China Town area during his visits there in the 1920's in his search for Shanghai Lil...

Ingredients:

4 X 275g / 10 oz Grey mullet, gutted and cleaned
300ml / 10 fl oz of good quality dry white wine
4 shallots, finely chopped
1 clove of garlic, crushed
a small bunch of fresh herbs
finely grated rind and juice of 1 lemon
a pinch of fresh nutmeg
3 anchovy fillets, roughly chopped
salt & freshly ground black pepper
2 tablespoon double cream mixed with 5ml / 1 teaspoon cornflour
sprig of fresh mint
slices of lemon and lemon zest

Method:

Pre-heat the oven to Gas mark 4, 350f/180c.

Put all the ingredients except the fresh mint into a large oven casserole and bake in the oven for 35 minutes.
Remove the mullet very carefully onto a warm serving dish and keep warm.
Bring the fish stock to the boil and reduce by half, simmering for 25 minutes, thicken with a little double cream mixed with cornflour.
Pour the sauce over the mullet garnished with a sprig of fresh mint and slices of lemon and zest.

ENGLISH KEDGEREE

Known as Kitchri and originally a spicy Indian recipe containing onions and lentils it was brought back to England for the Breakfast and Lunch table in the 18th century by the nabobs of the East India Company.
Finny 'Addy at its best...

Ingredients:

450g / 1 lb Cooked Finnan Haddock, bone & skin removed
175g / 6 oz Cooked long-grain rice
salt
freshly ground black pepper
saffron powder
3 eggs, hard boiled and shelled
2 tablespoon double cream
50g / 2 oz best butter
freshly chopped parsley
coriander leaves

Method:

Flake the cooked finnan haddock, making sure all the bones and skin are removed.
Melt the butter in medium saucepan, add the fish with a pinch of saffron.
Chop the eggs and add them with the rice to the saucepan.
Gently heat all the ingredients together, slowly add the cream, stirring thoroughly, season with salt and freshly ground black pepper and serve hot with a sprinkle of freshly chopped parsley or coriander leaves.

Serves: 6

OVEN BAKED SALMON

The best of British food with a garnish of Sweet Herb Creamed Potato mash, and Baked Bramley apple.

Ingredients:

4 x 225g / 8 oz Salmon fillet, scales and fins removed, skin on
50g / 2 oz melted butter

Dry Ingredients

salt
freshly milled black pepper
1 teaspoon crushed fennel seeds
4 tablespoon fresh breadcrumbs
1 tablespoon poppy seeds

4 small Bramley apples, cored and filled with a little grated nutmeg and a
sprig of mint and fennel
450g / 1lb boiled and creamed potato (hot)
1 teaspoon freshly ground mint and fennel, blended with the
creamed potato.
4 tablespoons melted butter
1 piping bag and star nozzle

Method:

Pre-heat the oven Gas 6, 200c/400f.

Grease a baking tray with the butter, place the salmon fillets, skin down
onto the baking tray, with the rest of the butter, and glaze the top of the
salmon.
Put all the dry ingredients into a bowl and mix them together.
Sprinkle them onto the salmon fillets.
Place the apples on the same tray and bake in the oven for 20 minutes.
Remove the salmon fillets onto a serving dish and return the apples to the
oven for a further 15 minutes until they are cooked.
Put the warmed creamed potato into a piping bag and pipe around the
salmon fillets, saving a little of the creamed potato to place the baked
apples onto, placing them near the salmon. Keep the salmon warm.
When the apples are cooked place them onto the corner of each piece of
salmon, pour over a tablespoon of the melted butter onto the salmon,
adding any of the juice on the baking tray.

FISH CAKES

Fish cakes should look like fish cakes and not tiny bite size morsels, that
you see on television, frozen from the packet and grilled or oven baked.
The flavour of the haddock, creamed potato and cheese send you into
orbit and a fish cake is not a fish cake without tomato sauce.

Ingredients:

50g / 2 oz butter
450g /1 lb Haddock or Cod fillet, poached, skin removed
450g /1 lb cooked and mashed potato
100g / 4 oz Wensleydale cheese, grated
1 large egg, blended with 1 tablespoon of cream
salt & freshly milled black pepper
1 tablespoon Worcestershire sauce
1 tablespoon anchovy essence
25g / 1 oz sifted flour on a saucer
1 egg whisked with a little milk
175g / 6 oz fine white breadcrumbs
50g / 2 oz beef dripping
1 sprig of fresh sage
1 lemon cut into wedges
1 bottle of thick tomato sauce

Method:

Melt the butter in a saucepan over a low heat and flake in the fish, beat in the potato, cheese and egg mixture. Season fish cake mixture with salt and freshly milled black pepper, finally add the Worcestershire sauce and anchovy essence.
Ensure that this mixture is completely blended.
Spread the mixture onto a floured surface to cool and with floured hands, form the mixture into 4-6 large fish cakes.
Dip the cakes into the egg wash and then into the breadcrumbs, repeat this process twice.
Fry the fish cakes in the hot dripping until golden brown for about 4 minutes either side. Serve with a fresh sage leaf, lemon wedge and some thick tomato sauce.

MUSHROOMS WITH ANCHOVY CREAM (1881 recipe)

Ingredients:

6 x 3-inch rounds of thick slice bread
50g / 2 oz beef dripping
225g / 8 oz wild mushrooms, chopped
10 chopped anchovies
3 tablespoons of thick double cream
salt & freshly milled black pepper

Method:

Fry the bread in the hot dripping, remove to a warm plate, fry the mushrooms for 4 minutes add the anchovies and cream and cook for a further 2 minutes season well and then spread onto the rounds of fried bread, serve hot.

TOM'S NUTS ABOUT HIS MUSHROOM & STILTON FRITTERS AND FRUITY ABOUT USING HIS LOAF

Ingredients:

450g / 1 lb even size white mushrooms
450g / 1 lb English Stilton Cheese
4 tablespoons vintage port
2 tablespoons crushed walnuts
125g / 5 oz seasoned plain flour
2 eggs beaten with a little milk
225g / 8 oz plain white breadcrumbs
75g / 3 oz crushed flaked almonds
1 Greenhalgh's fruit loaf
Shredded Red Velvet Beetroot
Garlic Mayonnaise
Beef dripping for frying or sunflower oil

Method:

Trim off the stalks to the mushrooms.
Mix together the Stilton, Port and walnuts.
Fill each mushroom with the Stilton filling.
Blend the breadcrumbs and almonds together.
Coat the mushrooms in the seasoned flour, then the egg & milk mixture,
finally into the breadcrumbs.
Heat the dripping or oil to 360f / 190 c and deep fry the mushrooms for
2 minutes until golden brown.
Slice the fruit loaf into $\frac{1}{2}$ inch slices and with a 4 inch round pastry
cutter, cut out several rounds of fruit loaf.
Place three mushrooms overlapping onto each round of fruit loaf and serve
with Shredded Red Velvet Beetroot and a garlic mayonnaise.

DENIS OLVERSTON'S WILD COUNTRY MUSHROOM OMELETTE

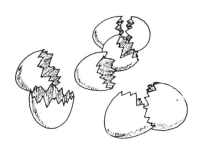

Ingredients:

50g / 2 oz butter
60ml / 2 fl oz olive oil
50g / 2 oz onion, chopped
75g / 3 oz spinach, washed and chopped
100g / 4 oz Wild mushrooms
1 teaspoon of fresh wild rosemary, crushed
salt
freshly milled black pepper
4 eggs, separated
grated Cheddar cheese
freshly chopped parsley

I suggest a warm, dark serving plate

Method:

In a sauté or small frying pan heat the butter and oil.
Fry the onion and spinach for about 3 minutes, add the mushrooms and rosemary and cook for a further 3 minutes.
Meanwhile beat the egg yolks in a mixing bowl and the whites in a separate bowl, season the egg yolks and blend carefully with the egg white.
Pour the egg mixture into the sauté pan slowly, stir the mixture, season and allow the omelette to cook on one side, add some grated cheese then brown under the grill, serve this onto a warm plate, sprinkled with chopped parsley.

BUTTON MUSHROOMS IN FENNEL SAUCE

This sauce acts as a marinade and then a sauce, served with new potatoes and braised celery these mushrooms will melt in your mouth.

Ingredients:

450g / 1 lb button mushrooms

MARINADE & SAUCE

150ml / 5 fl oz olive oil
2 teaspoons lemon juice
1 tablespoon white wine vinegar
large onion, chopped
1 teaspoon fennel seed, crushed
salt
freshly milled black pepper
2 tablespoons of port

Method:

Mix all the ingredients together in a bowl and leave the mixture to stand for 2 hours.
Add the mushrooms completely cover them with the marinade, chill for a further 2 hours.
Bring the sauce to the boil and reduce and simmer for 10 minutes.
Remove the mushrooms with a slotted spoon and pour over a little of the sauce and serve.

TB's BEEF WELLINGTON
with Lancashire Cheese and Mustard

I created this recipe for a dinner party and pie society meeting. It was a friend's birthday and we decided to come up with something completely different. With my addition of Lancashire cheese and mustard, it really is very tasty. This was then served with a Madeira sauce. For a quite normal beef Wellington omit the cheese and mustard.

Ingredients:

900g/ 2 lb fillet or Sirloin of Beef
75g / 3 oz butter
2 onions finely chopped
285g/ 10 oz button mushrooms or Wild mushrooms
900g / 2lb puff pastry
225g / 8 oz Chicken Liver Pate
225g / 8 oz Creamy Lancashire cheese, crumbled
4 tablespoon English mustard
1 egg, lightly beaten
salt
freshly ground black pepper

Method:

With a sharp knife, trim the fat from the beef fillet or sirloin.
Season the meat well with salt and ground black pepper.
Melt the butter in a large frying pan, add the beef, sealing the meat all over cooking for at least 10 minutes. Remove the fillet from the pan, placing it to one side.
In the same pan add a little more butter and add the chopped onion and mushrooms cooking until all the moisture has evaporated, allow them to cool.
Pre-set the Oven to Gas 6, 200c/400f.
Roll out the pastry to a large rectangle and place onto a greased baking sheet.
Spread the onion and mushroom mixture onto the centre of the pastry, place the beef onto the mixture. Top the fillet with a layer of pate.
cheese and mustard
Brush the edges of the pastry with the beaten egg, fold and seal the pastry, pressing the edges to seal the pastry.
Make some flowers and leaves from the leftover pastry and brush it completely with the beaten egg. Bake in the centre of the oven for 20 minutes, then lower the oven to Gas 4 350f/180c for a further 15 minutes until golden brown.
Serve with a Madeira sauce (next page)

Serves: 6-8

RUTH'S MADEIRA SAUCE

Ingredients:

6 Shallots, finely chopped
$\frac{1}{2}$ clove, crushed garlic
170g / 6 oz button mushrooms, chopped
half a bottle of Madeira Wine
60ml/ 4 tablespoon warm beef marrow
150ml/ $\frac{1}{4}$ pint of beef stock
5ml/ 1 teaspoon freshly chopped parsley
salt & freshly ground black pepper

Method:

Into a saucepan place a little butter, add the shallots, garlic and mushrooms and lightly blanch. Add the wine and cook until it is reduced to a third of the original quantity.
Add the beef stock and beef marrow, Season with salt and pepper.
Simmer for a further 20 minutes, add the parsley and serve with the Beef Wellington.

TOM, AMANDA'S AND BRENDA'S RATATOUILLE

Ingredients:

450g / 1 lb Aubergines
450g / 1 lb Tinned Chopped tomatoes
450g / 1 lb green and yellow courgettes
1 red pepper
1 yellow pepper
450g / 1 lb red onions
1 teaspoon of crushed garlic
120ml / 4 fl oz olive oil
50g / 2 oz tomato puree
sea salt and freshly ground black pepper
1 teaspoon of oregano
1 teaspoon of chopped basil

Method:

Cut the aubergines into 1 to 2 inch cubes and soak in salt water for 20 minutes. Slice the rest of the vegetable into thick chunks.
Heat the oil in a large deep pan and stir-fry the onion and garlic for about 4 minutes.
Add the rest of the vegetables and cook for 3 minutes, add the rest of the ingredients and cook for a further 3 minutes.
Tom's Tip: Pour the Ratatouille into a baking dish, sprinkle with grated cheese and bake in the oven for 15 minutes.

You know...... I should have been a chef...

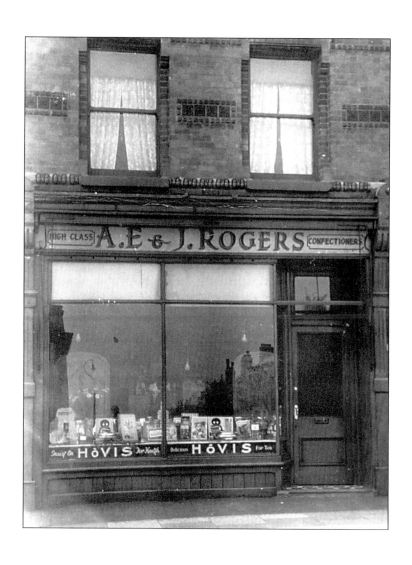

*Another bakery in King
Street Wallasey.*

*Owned and run by Ada
Elizabeth and Janet Frances
Rogers.*

*Photograph courtesy of Mrs
Adams of Wallasey.*

SECTION FIVE

WINTER WARMERS

Log and coal fires burning, friends coming to visit on a cold winters night...
The snow falls and chaos is brought to the roads, so we will need a flask
of hot soup to help dig and pull out the cars, sheep and cattle, or to clear
the snow from the driveway.

OXTAIL SOUP with FRESH TARRAGON DUMPLINGS

With several tinned and pre-packed varieties of oxtail soup the original
subtle taste is not well known to most of us .
Reg Williams is a regular listener from Birkenhead; he knows how to make
a Cornish Pasty, but can't make dumplings ... so here we are Reg, have a go.
The combination of fresh Oxtails and Tarragon Dumplings is something
that every lover of good British food should experience.
This recipe is made in two stages, but I am sure you will find it worth the
effort.
Should you have any problems getting hold of oxtails give your freindly
local butcher a call.... they'll do their best to get you sorted out.

Ingredients:

Stage One - Soup

1 whole Oxtail
50g / 2 oz Plain flour (seasoned)
1½ litres / 3 pints of beef stock
3 tablespoons of sunflower oil
1 large carrot
1 stick of celery
1 onion
small turnip
1 teaspoon thyme
1 bay leaf
110 ml / 4 fl oz Claret or Sherry
salt and freshly ground black pepper

Stage Two - Tarragon Dumplings

50g / 2 oz self raising flour
50g / 2 oz fresh breadcrumbs
2 tablespoons shredded suet
2 tablespoons of fresh tarragon leaves
2 tablespoons finely grated lemon rind
1 egg
salt & freshly ground black pepper

Method - Stage One:

Chop the oxtail into pieces through their natural joints, coating lightly with the seasoned flour.
Quickly fry them in a large deep saucepan in hot butter until they are lightly browned.
Peel and dice all the vegetables into 2.5cm (1 inch) squares.
Add the oil to the pan and brown them together.
Pour over the claret and add all the rest of the ingredients except the beef stock.
Cook for 10 minutes, then gradually add the beef stock.
Simmer for three hours, skimming of any excess fat, while simmering.
Strain off the liquid into large clean saucepan and allow it to cool.
Remove the oxtail meat and finely chop the meat returning it to the soup.
Re-boil and correct the seasoning; allow it to simmer while making the dumplings.

Method - Stage Two:

For the Tarragon dumplings. Mix together all the dry ingredients in a large clean bowl.
Add the egg and blend in thoroughly, add enough milk to make the dough moist, shape into small balls, roll them in a little flour and cook them for 10 minutes in boiling salted water.
Remove them carefully and add them to the soup.
Cook for a further 12 minutes.
Serve with a home-made crusty bread.

TOM'S COOKERY TIP

With the left over vegetables from the stock, mash them with a little butter, make them into little patties, dip them into the left over flour and fry them in a little butter and serve with your main course.

Serves: 6-8

PENNY'S SAVOURY MINCE DUMPLINGS

Garry Fields and his wife Penny live in Whitby, Ellesmere Port and they listen to the radio show every Wednesday and declared it Excellent ! Garry sent me a wonderful old recipe book (pre War) and I have taken some of the traditional Merseyside recipes from the book, so that you can also enjoy them.
Thank you Garry and Penny

Ingredients:

275g / 10 oz flour
1 pint of beef stock (cold)
1 teaspoon baking powder
450g / 1 lb minced steak
1 large onion chopped
225g / 8 oz shredded beef suet
salt & milled pepper
pepper

Method:

Sift the flour, salt and baking powder into a large basin.
Mix in the shredded suet, slowly add in enough cold stock to make a dumpling dough, which will not adhere to the fingers when touched.
Turn the dough out onto a floured board. Roll out.
Spread the minced steak and onion into the centre, season and roll up like roly poly or swiss roll style, wrap in well buttered greaseproof paper or a cloth and boil or steam for 2 hours.
Serve with boiled cabbage and a rich onion gravy.

BARLEY SOUP "RAM AY KISS STYLE"

Peter Ramejkis and his mother Lilly live in God's own country of Kirkby and they love their food. I had a great chat with Pete, who works for Sayers bakeries and like myself the smell of homely grub holds us down.

Ingredients:

1.5 pints / 900ml chicken stock
50g / 2 oz butter
450g / 1 lb mixed rabbit and chicken pieces
75g / 3 oz Barley, soaked for 3 hours in warm water and drained
1 carrot, diced, 1 onion, diced
75g / 3 oz diced turnip
1 large potato, diced
$\frac{1}{2}$ teaspoon of mixed herbs
salt and freshly milled black pepper

Method:

Make up the chicken stock or use a chicken stock cube.
Melt the butter in a large pan, cook the rabbit and chicken for 5 minutes, add the rest of the ingredients except the stock, cook for 15 minutes
Add the stock slowly and simmer for 30 minutes, let it stand for 15 minutes, then simmer again for 20 minutes with a lid and let the liquid reduce slightly. Let it stand for 10 minutes before serving with crusty bread.

LIVER, BACON & ONION BAKE

A survey was done in all the POSH restaurants and pubs all over England and this is the recipe that beat all the Nouvelle cuisine from restaurants across the country.

Ingredients:

8 smoked streaky bacon rashers, rindless and chopped
350g / 12 oz Lambs liver, finely sliced
25g / 1 oz best dripping
450g / 1 lb King Edward potatoes, sliced
450g / 1 lb onions, chopped
600ml / 1 pint beef stock
freshly milled black pepper
freshly chopped parsley
100g / 4 oz grated cheese

Method:

Melt the dripping in a large frying pan and cook the bacon and liver for 8 minutes. In a separate pan fry the potatoes and onion and cook for a further 12 minutes.
Place the liver and bacon into a ovenproof casserole dish, top with the potatoes and onion.
Add enough stock just to reach the base of the potatoes
Season and sprinkle with parsley and grated cheese.
Bake in the oven Gas mark 6, 200c, 400f for 25 minutes.

SEAN & WILLIE'S CHICKEN & LEEK SOUP

The twosome's recipe really makes this a main course soup. You can also add a little rice and peppers to bring out the colour should you wish to.

Ingredients:

30g/ 1 oz butter
350g / 12 oz uncooked chicken meat, bones removed
350g / 12 oz leeks, washed and cut into 2.5cm / 1 inch pieces
1200 ml / 2 pints chicken stock
1 bouquet garni sachet
salt
freshly milled white pepper
8 prunes, stoned and halved

Method:

Melt the butter in a large saucepan and fry off the chicken and leeks and fry for 8 minutes.
Add the stock and bouquet garni sachet, seasoning well to taste.
Bring the soup to the boil and simmer for 45 minutes.
Add the prunes with a little rice and diced peppers if you wish and simmer for 20 minutes.

Serves: 6

AUNTY DOREEN'S LIVERPOOL MIST

A foggy night in Park Lane, Bootle caused this thick misty soup recipe to be created.

Ingredients:

450g / 1 lb Leeks, trimmed, sliced and washed
25g / 1 oz butter
350g / 12 oz onions (Spanish) chopped
2 celery sticks, chopped
2 tablespoon (each) rice and split peas
1200ml / 2 pints lamb stock
salt
freshly milled black pepper
100ml / 4 fl oz double cream
chives

Method:

Melt the butter in a large saucepan, add the leeks, onion and celery, and cook gently for 10 minutes.
Add the rice, split peas and lamb stock, simmering for 40 minutes.
Season to taste, add the cream, reheat and serve with chopped chives.

Serves: 4-6

PEA WACK

I am not a Scouser, but my wife and boys are, so surely this makes me an honorary Scouser! Considering I'm giving you my Scouse recipe for Pea wack, I should at least be known as Wack Bridge for giving you the true flavour of this soup.
To add extra zest serve this with the Dumplings from the Oxtail recipe on page 77.

Ingredients:

3 rashers of smoked, rindless streaky bacon, diced
1 large onion, chopped
small knob of butter
450g / 1 lb ready soaked peas
225g / 8 oz cubed York ham
2.3 litres / 4 pints of chicken stock
salt
freshly milled black pepper
150ml / 5 fl oz double cream
chopped parsley
croutons

Method:

Put the bacon and onion into a large saucepan with a little butter and cook over a gentle heat for 6 minutes.
Add the peas, ham and the stock to the pan, bring to the boil, season lightly with salt and freshly milled black pepper, cover and simmer for 2 hours.
Add the cream and blend thoroughly, sprinkle with parsley and top with cheesy croutons.

Tom's Tip: Some cooks strain this soup, if you let it stand and allow the peas to dry out, they can then be blended and used to thicken vegetable soup and stews.

Serves: 4-6

POTATO AND ONION BAKE

Ingredients:

6 large baking potatoes, peeled and finely sliced
2 large onions. peeled and finely sliced
100g / 4 oz Cheshire Cheese, grated
100g / 4 oz leeks, finely cut
salt
freshly ground black pepper
150ml / $\frac{1}{4}$ pint of milk, blended with 1 egg
4 tablespoons vegetable stock

Method:

Pre heat the oven to 200c / 400F / Gas mark 6
In a large, shallow, ovenproof dish, alternate the potatoes, onion, cheese and leeks, seasoning each layer.

Pour over the blended milk and egg, and the vegetable stock.
Cover and bake in the oven for 40 minutes.

Remove the cover and bake for a further 10 minutes.
Brown to taste.

POACHERS' PIE

I love game pies and this one is the best of British.
If you have problems buying game where you live try Scott's Butchers of
Ormskirk who'll be only too pleased to help you out.

Ingredients:

225g / 8 oz boneless rabbit, skinned and cubed
225g / 8 oz boneless grouse, skin removed and cubed
225g / 8 oz boneless pheasant, skin removed and cubed
100g / 4 oz rindless streaky bacon, chopped
1 large leek, sliced and washed
1 tablespoon freshly chopped parsley
chicken stock

Pastry

225g / 8 oz plain flour
salt and freshly milled white pepper
50g / 2 oz butter
50g / 2 oz lard
1 egg to glaze

Method:

Pre-heat the oven to Gas mark 5 , 190C/375F.

Fill a large pie dish with alternative layers of the game, bacon, vegetables,
seasoning well, adding the herbs and just enough chicken stock to half fill
the pie dish.
To make the pastry put the flour and a little seasoning into a bowl. Rub in
the butter and lard until the mixture resembles fine breadcrumbs, adding
enough cold water, about 60ml / 4 tablespoon, mixing to form a very firm
dough.
Roll out the pastry on a lightly floured surface to cover the pie dish.
Trim and seal the edges, making a small hole in the centre to let out the
steam. Brush the top with the egg.
Bake in the oven for 35 minutes. Cover loosely with greased baking foil,
reducing the heat to gas mark 4, 180C/350F for one hour.

Serves: 8

ROSIE'S ROAST LAMB WITH ROSEMARY AND HONEY SAUCE

Courtesy of Rosie B. from St.Helens for this one.

Try this recipe with Sage and marmalade, coated on the lamb before baking as an alternative to the Rosemary and Honey sauce.

Ingredients:

3 lb / 1 leg of lamb, boned and rolled
salt
freshly milled black pepper
2 cloves crushed garlic
1 teaspoon paprika
3 fresh sprigs of rosemary, soaked in 6 tablespoons of fresh orange juice
6 tablespoons clear honey
1 tablespoon of freshly chopped mint
150ml / 5 fl oz beef stock
1 tablespoon of cornflour mixed with a little orange juice

Method:

Pre-heat the oven to Gas 6, 200c/ 400f.
Rub the lamb with the salt, pepper, garlic and paprika and cook in the oven for 30 minutes.
Place the rest of the ingredients except the cornflour into a saucepan and bring to the boil then simmer for 15 minutes.
Thicken with the cornflour.
Baste the meat with the rosemary and honey sauce every 15 minutes for 1 hour.
Remove the lamb to a large serving plate, carve and add the juices to the rest of the rosemary and honey sauce.
Serve with the sauce and new potatoes and fresh winter cabbage.

Serves: 4- 6

ENGLAND'S ROAST SIRLOIN OF BEEF WITH A HERB STUFFING

Yes an English name and from English butchers of extremely high quality. Knighted in Lancashire it might have been, but the Sir-Loin of beef is not a recipe to be left out of any good cookbook, especially in Winter.

Ingredients:
25g / 1 oz beef dripping
4 shallots, roughly chopped
50g / 2 oz wild mushrooms, finely chopped
1 teaspoon of dried tarragon
1 teaspoon of dried parsley
50g / 2 oz fresh brown breadcrumbs
2 sprigs of fresh thyme
salt
freshly milled black pepper
1 egg, blended with 1 tablespoon port
2 tablespoons double cream
1kg / 2 lb sirloin steak, in one piece
6 Jacket potatoes, washed and pricked all over

Method:

Pre-heat the oven gas 6, 200c/400f.

Melt the dripping in a large saucepan and fry the shallots, and mushrooms for 5 minutes.
Remove the pan from the heat and blend all the ingredients, except the egg and cream.
Thoroughly blend them and allow the stuffing to cool, add the remaining ingredients, ensuring the mixture is completed binded.
Place the steak on a board with the meat on the board and the fat facing you. Insert a sharp knife into the middle of the steak and slice horizontally to within 2.5cm / 1 inch of the end of the steak, to make a pocket.
Place the stuffing inside the steak, covering the whole length of the sirloin.
Sew up the pocket with butchers string or thick cotton. Place the steak onto a large baking tray, with the jacket potatoes holding the meat, 3 on each side of the beef. Bake in the centre of the oven for 1 hour .
Place the meat onto a serving dish, remove the string and carve into generous thick slices.
Serve with Yorkshire pudding (page 98), baked parsnips, cauliflower cheese and jacket potatoes.

Serves: 6

TRADITIONAL ENGLISH STEAK & KIDNEY PIE

Everyones favourite and the most popular pie around Great Britain, not only in the households but restaurants, cafes and hotels around the world. Do not substitute cheap cuts of meat use the best Rump Steak and Ox kidney to achieve the perfect pie.
Should you want to make this into a STEAK & ALE, then omit the kidney and soak the steak in 150ml / 5 fl oz beer overnight, then use the beer with the stock.

Ingredients:

575g / 1.25 lb Rump Steak
175g / 6 oz ox kidney
1 Large onion
300ml / ½ pint Beef stock
25g / 1 oz seasoned flour
225g / 8 oz Suet Crust Pastry
25g / 1 oz butter
salt & freshly milled black pepper

Method:

Trim the Steak of the skin and fat and dice into 2.5cm/ 1 inch cubes.
Remove the fat, skin and core from the kidney and dice this quite small.
Toss the steak and kidney into the seasoned flour.
Into a large frying pan melt the butter and quickly seal the meat all over, adding the chopped onion cooking for 4 minutes.
Add the beefstock season and simmer for a further 25 minutes.
While the beef is simmering, line a large well-greased pudding basin with the suet crust pastry, leaving enough pastry to make a lid.
Put the steak, kidney and stock into the basin and top with the lid, damping the edges with water to make it stick.
Cover the basin with buttered tin foil or greaseproof paper.
Stand the basin in a large saucepan with enough water to half cover the basin.
Finally bring the water to the boil and steam for 2 hours, making sure you top up the water, so the pan will not dry.
Serve with fresh carrots & swede mashed with a little butter and nutmeg, garnished with roast potatoes.

Serves: 6

MAKENTIE CHICKEN AND BROCCOLI PIE

I spent some of the best years of my life developing pies for a famous
Northern pie manufacturers. This recipe is from my home village of
Newburgh in North West Lancashire; in Wales they use leeks instead of
broccoli and in Ireland they use potatoes.
The only way to get the best results from this type of pie is to have a
shortcrust base with a puff pastry topping.

Ingredients:

50g / 2 oz butter
2 carrots diced very fine
8 shallots, skinned and sliced
100g / 4 oz button mushrooms
25g / 1 oz plain flour
300ml / 10 fl oz fresh milk
150ml /5 fl oz double cream
450g / 1 lb chicken breast, cooked and diced
175g / 6 oz broccoli florets, blanched
50g / 2 oz cheddar cheese, grated
salt & freshly milled black pepper
175g / 6 oz shortcrust pastry for the base and 100g / 4 oz puff pastry
for the top
1 egg for glazing

Method:

Pre-heat the oven to Gas 6, 400f / 200c

Melt the butter in a large saucepan and fry gently the carrots, shallots
and button mushrooms for about 10 minutes, stirring with a wooden
spoon occasionally.
Add the flour and cook for a further 2 minutes, gradually add the warm
milk and cream, stirring continuously until the sauce becomes thick and
creamy, simmering for 2 minutes.
Add the chicken, broccoli and grated cheese to the sauce, seasoning well
with salt and freshly milled black pepper and allow the mixture to cool.
Roll out the short pastry base and line a greased ovenproof pie dish with
the pastry.
Pour in the cool mixture and top with puff pastry and bake in the centre
of the oven for 30 minutes.
Serve this sumptuous pie with baked parsnips and creamed potatoes to
soak up the very creamy sauce.

GROUSE PIE

In Scotland and Lancashire grouse pie is always served with fried bread and Rowan jelly. True to form of a good chef I have combined these ingredients into this truly traditional Grouse Pie.

Ingredients:

1 tablespoon cooking oil
25g / 1 oz butter
450g / 1 lb grouse meat
salt
freshly milled black pepper
6 slices rindless streaky bacon, finely chopped
8 shallots, peeled and sliced
1 small carrot diced
85ml /3 fl oz red wine
150ml / 5 fl oz chicken stock
2 tablespoons of double cream
5 tablespoons rowan jelly (see page 116)
2 tablespoons fresh parsley
275g / 10 oz puff pastry

Method:

Pre-heat the oven to gas mark 6, 200c/400f.

Melt the butter with the cooking oil in a large saucepan, add the grouse meat and seal the meat all over, season with salt and pepper, simmering for 3 minutes, add the bacon, shallots and carrot, stirring briskly for a further 3 minutes.
Add the wine and chicken stock bring to the boil and simmer for 25 minutes on a low heat, reducing the stock by at least one third.
Allow the grouse and sauce to cool slightly and blend in the double cream and rowan jelly.
Roll out the pastry to fit a 1200 ml/ 2 pint, pie dish.
Place the mixture into the pie dish, sprinkle with freshly chopped parsley and place on the puff pastry lid.
Wash the top with a little milk and bake in the centre of the oven for 25 minutes.
Next use 2 slices of white bread cut into quarters
25g / 1 oz olive oil & 25g / 1 oz butter

Fry the bread in the hot oil and butter and place around the pie when it is ready to be served.

Serves: 4-6

SNELLY JUNIOR'S SHEPHERDS PIE

By the time this book is published Calum Snell will be nearly two years old and daddy big burly Snelly will be feeding him some of my favourite recipes like this one .
How many arguments have I had over this pie? If I had a pint for every argument, I would own a brewery !
Shepherds Pie is made with Lamb and Cottage Pie with Beef.
I do feel that the meat must be cooked for a shepherds pie and that is the first stage; I have also added extra flavours.
I found the original recipes very bland including Mrs Beeton's from 1861.
It is always sprinkled with Lancashire or Cheshire cheese before baking.

Ingredients:

25g / 1 oz beef dripping
450g / 1 lb roughly minced lamb
225g / 8 oz loin lamb, fat removed and diced
2 large onions, skinned and sliced
2 carrots, peeled and diced
a pinch of fresh rosemary
salt
freshly milled black pepper
25g / 1 oz plain flour
300ml / 10 fl oz lamb stock
2 tablespoons port
1 tablespoon Worcestershire sauce
1 tablespoon tomato puree
100g / 4 oz sweet peas
700g / 1½ lb warm mashed potato, seasoned buttered
25g / 1 oz butter, softened
75g / 3 oz crumbly Lancashire cheese

Method:

Pre-heat the oven to Gas 6, 400f / 200c.

Melt the dripping in a large saucepan and fry the lamb for 10 minutes, add the onions, carrots and rosemary, fry for a further 5 minutes, season with salt and pepper.
Add the flour and cook for a further two minutes, very slowly add the stock and port, finally add the Worcestershire sauce and tomato puree and cook for a further 25 minutes , stirring every 4 minutes . Blend in the peas and allow the mixture to cool.
Place the mixture into a deep pie dish and cover with warm mashed potato, using a fork to spread the potato ensuring every area is completely covered.
Sprinkle with softened butter and the crumbled Lancashire cheese and bake in the centre of the oven for 20 minutes.

SPENCER'S COTTAGE PIE

You really do have to listen to 'On the Beat' and 'On the Mersey Beat' when making this awesome recipe of Spencer Leigh's, it should be made while Spence is making and talking music.

Ingredients:

25g / 1 oz beef dripping
450g / 1 lb roughly minced Beef
225g / 8 oz Rump steak, diced
1 large onion, skinned and sliced
1 large carrot, peeled and diced
a pinch of fresh thyme
salt
freshly milled black pepper
25g / 1 oz plain flour
300ml / 10 fl oz Beef stock
1 tablespoon Worcestershire sauce
1 tablespoon tomato puree
700g / 1½ lb warm mashed potato, seasoned buttered
25g / 1 oz butter, softened

Method:

Pre-heat the oven to Gas 6, 400f / 200c.

Melt the dripping in a large saucepan and fry the beef for 10 minutes, add the onions, carrot and thyme, fry for a further 5 minutes, season with salt and pepper.
Add the flour and cook for a further two minutes, very slowly add the beef stock, finally add the Worcestershire sauce and tomato puree and cook for a further 25 minutes, stirring every 4 minutes, allow the mixture to cool.
Place the mixture into a deep pie dish and cover with warm mashed potato, using a fork to spread the potato ensuring every area is completely covered.
Sprinkle with softened butter and bake in the centre of the oven for 25 minutes.

NOBBY'S SPUD PIE

This is one of those recipes that I had passed onto me by my dad Nobby, an ex-soldier (Liverpool Kings Division) he so loved home-cooked food and he had is very special way of cooking. If you could put a spoon in his 'Tattie' pie mixture and it fell over it wasn't thick enough !
That's a dad for ya !

Ingredients:

25g / 1 oz beef dripping
700g / 1½ lb roughly minced beef
900g / 2 lb potatoes, peeled and diced
150g / 5 oz diced carrot
225g / 8 oz sliced onion
1 tablespoon mixed herbs
25g / 1 oz plain flour
100g / 4 oz marrowfat peas
300ml / 10 fl oz beef stock
salt
freshly milled black pepper
225g /8 oz black pudding, skin removed and diced
Pastry as for Poachers's Pie (page 84)
fresh milk, to glaze

Method:

Pre-heat the oven to gas mark 6, 200c/400f.

Into a large saucepan heat the dripping until it is quite hot, add the mince and very quickly seal and brown it for 5 minutes, add the potatoes, carrot, onion and mixed herbs, cooking for 4 minutes, sprinkle with the flour, stir, add the peas and beef stock bring to the boil and simmer for 15 minutes, season with salt and freshly milled black pepper. Put the mixture into a 1200 ml / 2 pint pie dish. Scattering the diced black pudding over the top (this helps to thicken the pie during the cooking process)
Make up the pastry as for game pie, cover the pie dish, sealing and crimping the pastry all around.
Trim of any excess pastry and decorate with pastry leaves.
Brush with milk and bake in the centre of the oven for 30-45 minutes.

Serves: 6.- 8

TOM'S CORNED BEEF & BEETROOT PIE

Princes foods in Liverpool make the best corned beef and I am sure you know it's very good for the lead in the pencil ! And Red Velvet Beets are a great blood purifier!

Ingredients:

25g / 1 oz beef dripping
450g / 1 lb roughly chopped Princes Corned Beef
225g / 8 oz Red Velvet Beetroot diced
1 large onion, skinned and sliced
1 carrot, peeled and diced
salt
freshly milled black pepper
25g / 1 oz plain flour
150ml / 5 fl oz lamb stock
2 tablespoons port
100g / 4 oz sweet peas
700g / 1½ lb warm mashed potato, seasoned buttered
25g / 1 oz butter, softened
75g / 3 oz crumbly Lancashire cheese

Method:

Pre-heat the oven to Gas 6, 400f / 200c.
Melt the dripping in a large saucepan and fry the corned beef for 2 minutes, add the beetroot, onion and carrot and fry for a further 5 minutes, season with salt and pepper.
Add the flour and cook for a further two minutes, very slowly add the stock and port, finally cook for a further 5 minutes , stirring well, blend in the peas and allow the mixture to cool.
Place the mixture into a deep pie dish and cover with warm mashed potato, using a fork to spread the potato ensuring every area is completely covered.
Sprinkle with softened butter and the crumbled Lancashire cheese and bake in the centre of the oven for 20 minutes.

MEAT PIE or MEAT PASTIE

Traditional food, made with extra special care for Merseyside folk.

Ingredients:

50g / 2 oz good beef dripping
900g / 2 lb of best British beef, roughly minced
3 onions, skinned and finely chopped
Salt
Freshly milled black pepper
570ml / 1 pint good beef stock
450g / 1 lb shortcrust pastry
Beaten egg and a little milk

Method:

Put the dripping into a large frying pan and melt, add the roughly minced beef, cook and brown for 12 minutes, add the onion, seasoning well and cook for a further 5 minutes, add the beef stock and simmer for 20 minutes stirring every three minutes. Allow the minced beef to cool.

For a Meat Pie

Roll out the pastry on a floured surface, using two-thirds for the base and putting the rest to one side for the topping. Grease and line the pie dish with the pastry. Place the meat mixture into the line pie dish and top with the remaining pastry. Trim and glaze and bake in the oven for 35 minutes until golden brown.

For Meat Pasties

Roll out the pastry to 6mm / ¼ inch in thickness and cut out eight x 15cm/ 6 inch rounds.

Place the meat mixture into the centre of each round, dampen the edges of each round and fold them over to make a half moon shape, pinch and crimp the edges. Glaze with the beaten egg and put the pasties onto a greased baking sheet.

And bake at gas mark 4, 180c/350f for 35 minutes.

Tom's Tip: Mix 1 tablespoon gelatine powder with 56ml of port and 300ml of beef stock and bring to the boil and reduce this by half (150ml), allow it to cool slightly then when the pies and pasties are cooked, pour in a little of the port gelatine liquid inside the pies or pasties, these are excellent cold and served with pickles.
Place them onto some kitchen paper to drain, keep them warm. Repeat the process and then sprinkle with Raspberry Vinegar, Cayenne pepper, garnish with lemon slices and sprigs of fresh mint.
Serve with slices of brown bread and butter with a glass of dry white wine.

Serves: 6-8

CORNED BEEF PUDDING

Mrs Melia from Old Swan asked for this recipe.

Ingredients:

350g / 12 oz Corned beef, cut into small cubes
1 small onion, finely chopped
Yorkshire pudding batter

Method:

Pre-heat the Oven to 220c / 425f, gas reg 7.
Fry the corned beef and onion in a little dripping for 3 minutes.
Place a large baking tray and the fat from the corned beef into the oven
for 3 minutes until it is very hot, the fat should be smoking.

Pour over the batter and sprinkle with the corned beef and onion.
Bake for 30 minutes and serve with a tomato sauce.

Serves: 4

TRADITIONAL TOXTETH TOAD

The word toad is popular all over England for a quick and simple lunch or
supper, if you don't like beef, try it with your favourite cut of meat,
poultry, game or the famous Banger, ensuring that the meat is at least
half cooked before you cook for the final 20 minutes.

Ingredients:

25g / 1 oz dripping
350g / 12 oz Sirloin steak, fat and gristle removed and cubed
salt
freshly milled black pepper
Yorkshire pudding batter

Method:

Pre-heat the oven to gas mark 8, 230c/450f

Heat the dripping in a baking tin until it is just smoking.
Pour in a quarter of the batter and bake for 10 minutes until the batter is
just set. While the batter is baking, season the meat and lightly fry the
meat until the batter is set, add the meat to the baking tin, pour in the
remainder of the batter and return to the oven and bake for 20 minutes .
Lower the heat (without opening the oven) to 200c / 400f, gas 6 for 15
minutes.
Serve with a red wine sauce or onion gravy.

Serves: 4

KNOTTY ASH FRUITY FRITTERS

You can visit the Jam butty mines in Knotty Ash and get some Jam Butties
and dip them in this sweet batter.
A recipe fit for a sailor, yes my Father-in-law Jim Fitzpatrick loved these
and this is a recipe taught to me by my Gran back in the 1960's when the
Beatles headlined everywhere including their home city.

Now where was that then ?

Ingredients:

25g / 1 oz yeast
150ml / 5 fl oz warm milk
225g / 8 oz plain flour
50g / 2 oz currants
50g / 2 oz caster sugar
2 medium sized apples, cored, peeled and grated
25g / 1 oz candied peel
a pinch freshly grated nutmeg
2 large eggs, whisked with a tablespoon of sherry
50g / 2 oz beef dripping
25g / 1 oz butter

Method:

Into a large bowl put the yeast and warm milk, whisk until it dissolves,
then leave it to stand for a few minutes.

Sift the flour with all the other dry ingredients into another bowl, Add
the eggs and blend, slowly add enough milk to make a thick paste, slowly
adding the milk to make a creamy batter.
Let the batter stand for at least 24 hours before using.
Slowly whisk the batter.

Heat the dripping and butter in a large pan until it is hot, adding 1
tablespoon of the fritters at a time to the hot fat. Fry for 2 minutes
either side until golden brown, drain onto some clean kitchen towel,
sprinkle with sugar and serve them warm.

THE SEQUENCE DANCER'S GUIDE TO BREAD PUDDING

*This one is for the gentleman who wrote to me explaining that he had to
have his b & b pudding before he could dance properly.
In honour of our friends from 'The Time of their Lives' feature every
Thursday at 10 to 2 on Roger Phillips' programme, courtesy of the
Liverpool Senior Citizens Forum.*

Ingredients:

25g / 1 oz butter
12 slices of bread
100g / 4 oz sultanas
20g / 2 oz currants
1 teaspoon freshly ground nutmeg
600ml / 20 fl oz milk
3 eggs
50g / 2 oz soft brown sugar
grated nutmeg
brown sugar

Method:

Pre-heat the oven gas 4, 180c /350f.

Grease a large baking dish (2 litre/ 3½ pints) with 25g / 1 oz butter.
Cut the bread into triangles and arrange in alternative layers, sprinkled
with sultanas and currants and grated nutmeg, finishing with a top layer of
bread in a neat pattern.
Heat the milk in a saucepan, do not let it boil.
Beat the eggs in a bowl with the sugar, whisk in the hot milk.
Strain the custard mixture over the bread, finish with a little more
grated nutmeg and a little more brown sugar.
Leave the dish to stand for 45 minutes.
Bake in the centre of the oven for 35-40 minutes until the custard is set.
Meanwhile have a quick dance and enjoy my recipe

Serves: 8

MRS E TANFIELD'S COLLEGE PUDDING

This is all down to the A-TEAM , yes they rang me and said Tom, Mrs Tanfield wants ya College Pudding recipe. So if you want anything at all call the A-Team on 0151 794 0984 and mention my name...

Ingredients:

Butter for greasing
100g / 4 oz plain flour
$\frac{1}{2}$ teaspoon baking powder
pinch of salt
$\frac{1}{4}$ teaspoon mixed spice
100/ 4 oz stale white breadcrumbs
75g / 3 oz shredded suet
75g/ 3 oz caster sugar
50g / 2 oz currants
50g / 2 oz sultanas
2 eggs beaten
100ml / 4 fl oz fresh milk

Method:

Grease 6 to 8 dariole moulds, set the oven at 190c / 375 f / gas 5.
Sift the flour, baking powder, salt and spice into a mixing bowl.
Add the crumbs, suet, sugar, currants and sultanas, and mix well.
Stir in the eggs with enough milk to form a soft dropping consistency.
Half fill the prepared dariole moulds with the mixture and bake in the centre of the oven for 20 to 25 minutes.

THE PERFECT YORKSHIRE PUDDING

Ingredients:

30ml (2 tbsp) beef dripping
100g (4 oz) Plain flour (sifted)
a pinch of salt
1 fresh (large) egg
200ml (7 fl oz) fresh milk
100mi (3 fl oz) water

Method:

Pre - heat the oven to gas 7, 425f, 220c into a clean bowl, mix the flour and a pinch of salt, make a well in the centre and break in the egg.
Add half the milk, using a wooden spoon, work in the flour slowly.
Beat the mixture until it is smooth, then add the remaining milk and the 100ml of water.
Beat until it is well mixed.
Put the dripping from the beef into a large baking tin or individual yorkshire pudding tray until the fat is very hot (smoking). Pour the batter and return to the oven to cook for 35
40 minutes, until risen and golden brown.
DO NOT OPEN THE OVEN DOOR AT ALL FOR AT LEAST 30 MINUTES.

SECTION SIX

CHRISTMAS IS COMING

The build up to the Christmas dinner must be an enjoyable but very light Christmas Breakfast and typical of everyone having a really enjoyable Christmas Eve. A fantasia of fun festive food with a sense of Northern flavours: Set out all the main courses on a buffet table, so that every-one can help themselves to a little of what they fancy.

CHAMPAGNE FRUIT SALAD

If you are making this for a buffet and at least 12 people, simply double the quantity.

Ingredients:

3 mandarins, peeled
1 kiwi fruit, peeled and chopped
1 banana, peeled and chopped
1 pear, peeled, cored and diced
1 apple, peeled, cored and diced
2 plums, sliced and pitted
225g / 8 oz seedless grapes, sliced
100g / 4 oz fresh strawberries, hulled and sliced
2 tablespoon brandy
2 tablespoon lemon juice
150ml / 5 fl oz Champagne

Method:

Put the segments of mandarin into a fruit bowl, with all the other fruits, add the brandy, lemon juice and champagne. Chill for 1 hour and serve into individual glass dishes with a sprig of fresh mint.

Serves: 6

AMANDA'S SMOKED SALMON with SCRAMBLED EGGS

Bit of a posh bird who works for Norman & Brian Olverson at Red Velvet Beetroot, in Scarisbrick. She's always chatting me up ! (I will have to give in some time).
This is also nice with bits of Brie dropped in !

Ingredients & Method:

Beat 2 eggs per person, seasoned with salt and freshly milled black pepper.
Melt a small walnut of butter, 1 tablespoon into a saucepan over a gentle heat, add the eggs stirring all the time with a wooden spoon. Add 50g / 2 oz smoked salmon cut into small diamonds per person.
Take the pan from the heat, add a little more butter with 1 tablespoon double cream and serve with a sprig of freshly snipped parsley and lightly buttered warm brown toast.

YO YO's SUPREME OF DUCKLING IN ORANGE BRANDY SAUCE
Courtesy of Yvonne Olverson
Makes a nice change from Turkey and is easier to cook

Ingredients:

50g / 2 oz butter
2 tablespoon olive oil
25g / 1 oz plain flour
8 x 225g / 8 oz Duckling Supreme
2 tablespoon chopped fresh tarragon
150ml / 5 fl oz fresh orange juice
3 fresh oranges cut into segments and rind cut into very fine strips (julienne)
50g / 2 oz courgettes, cut into very fine strips
50g / 2 oz red peppers, cut into very fine strips
50/ 2 oz shredded leeks
150ml / 5 fl oz Orange Brandy
salt and freshly milled black pepper
150ml /5 fl oz Fromage frais

Method:

Heat the butter and oil in a large frying pan, add the duck supremes and cook quickly until light golden brown all over.
Add the Orange brandy and cook for 2 minutes, sprinkle lightly with the flour and cook for a further minute.
Reduce the heat and add the Orange juice, courgettes, peppers and leeks, season with salt and freshly milled black pepper, simmer for 4 minutes until the orange sauce is reduced and thickens.
Add half the segments, rind, tarragon and fromage frais cook for a further 2 minutes.

Slice the duck breasts into thin segments and fan it around the centre of a large warm plate, with a little sauce, garnished with segments of orange and fresh tarragon leaves, sprinkle the fanned supremes with fresh strips of orange rind.

Serves: 8

BREAST OF QUAIL FILLED WITH DUCK LIVERS, PORT & MUSHROOMS
In a Cream & Honey Sauce

Garnished with holly and mistletoe, this cannot help to bring a ray of Christmas spirit to the dining table.
This one is for Eddie Johnson of Kensington.

Ingredients:

16 Quails cooked for 15 minutes and boned
16 soft boiled Quail Eggs
50g / 2 oz butter
225g / 8 oz Duck livers
175g / 6 oz chopped Mushrooms
175g / 6 oz chopped Onions
4 tablespoon Port
4 tablespoon dry red wine
2 tablespoon warm honey
3 tablespoon fromage frais
salt
freshly milled black pepper
blackcurrants

Method:

Joint and bone the quail breasts, remove the meat. Put the butter into a large saucepan (sauté), and cook the duck livers for 1 minute, add the onion and mushrooms.
Season well with salt and freshly milled black pepper.
Add the port, red wine and quail meat, allowing it to simmer for 6 minutes.
Pour over the honey and fromage frais, blend and let it simmer for a further 2 minutes.
Garnish the warm plates with the quail eggs cut into halves with a few berries.
Place a large pastry cutter into the centre of each plate, filling it with the livers, mushroom, onion and sauce.
Remove the cutter and top the filling with Quail meat, topped with a soupcon of sauce.
Serves: 8

BRAISED PORK FILLET WITH RED CABBAGE

The flavours from the pork cooking with the red cabbage are so unusual, that this recipe alone deserves to have its place in the history of British cookery.

Ingredients:

4 x 450g / 1 lb pork fillets, in one piece
3 tablespoons , sesame oil
25g / 1 oz butter
12 shallots, peeled
2 cloves garlic
3 sprigs of rosemary, finely chopped
6 chestnuts , peeled and chopped
450g / 1 lb red cabbage, very finely shredded
salt
freshly milled black pepper
150ml / 5 fl oz sweet cider
2 sprigs of fresh thyme

Method:

Pre-heat the oven gas mark 5, 190c/375f

Clean the pork fillets, remove any excess fat. Put the oil and butter into a large frying pan and seal the pork fillets cooking quickly all over for 4 minutes. Remove the fillets and place them in a deep oven casserole.
Add the shallots, garlic, rosemary and chestnuts to the frying pan and cook them for 5 minutes and then place them with the pork.
Quickly fry the red cabbage in the same pan for 6 minutes, seasoning well with salt and freshly milled black pepper.
Add the cider and cook for a further 8 minutes. Place the cabbage and all the juices over the pork fillets to completely cover them.
Place the 2 sprigs of thyme onto the cabbage, cover with tin foil and braise in the centre of the oven for 35 minutes.

Remove the foil and discard the thyme , place the red cabbage with a slotted spoon onto a large serving dish.
Slice the pork fillets and lay on the top of the cabbage, garnished with the shallots.
Served with sweet snow peas, garnished with fresh watercress.

Serves: 8- 10

ROAST TURKEY WITH ORANGE AND LEMON STUFFING

I know that every one likes Turkey at Christmas time, but have you ever had Turkey made with my favourite stuffing... St. Clements?

Ingredients:

4.5 kg / 10 lb oven -ready turkey
100g / 4 oz melted butter
juice of 1 lemon
juice of 1 orange
5 tablespoons sweet white wine
2 tablespoons of freshly chopped mint

LEMON AND ORANGE STUFFING

50g / 2 oz butter
4 tablespoons of shallots, finely chopped
1 tablespoon freshly chopped rosemary
2 tablespoons of chestnut puree
500g / 1 lb Cumberland sausage meat
Juice, finely grated rind of 2 lemons and 2 oranges
100g / 4 oz fresh brown breadcrumbs
2 tablespoons fresh parsley finely chopped
salt & freshly milled black pepper
10 mini pork sausages
10 small slices, rindless streaky bacon
3 oranges
3 lemons
2 sprigs of parsley

Method:

Pre-heat the oven gas mark 7, 220c/425f.

For the lemon and orange stuffing:
Fry the shallots in the butter for 2 minutes, add the rosemary and chestnut puree and cook for a further 3 minutes.
Put all the other stuffing ingredients into a large bowl and blend all together with the shallot mixture and butter.
Stuff the neck end of the turkey, truss and place the turkey on a rack in a large roasting tin.
Put the butter, lemon, orange, wine and mint into a bowl and baste the turkey with the marinade every 20 minutes.
Place the turkey in the oven and cook for 30 minutes, lower the heat to gas mark 4, 180c/350f and cook for 3 hours. During the last 30 minutes place the sausages and bacon around the turkey.
Serve with a giblet gravy made from the turkey and basting juices.
Garnish with mini pork sausages wrapped in streaky bacon, garnished with crowns of orange and lemon.

Serves: 10

BRIAN's PAN-FRIED FILLET STEAK
WITH OYSTER MUSHROOMS & RED VELVET BEETROOT

Brian's a great bloke who lets me play with his beetroots now and again...
so when pan frying the steak, throw in a couple of beets, they are 'brill'
fried with mushrooms.
I am sure that during the Christmas period everyone does get fed up of
Turkey and another festive recipe would be welcomed. This is one of those
recipes that is welcomed everywhere.

Ingredients:

6 X 225g / 8 oz fillet steaks, trimmed of all fat
salt
freshly milled black pepper
25g / 1 oz butter
2 tablespoons olive oil
75ml / 3 fl oz port
75ml / 3 fl oz beef stock
3 tablespoons English mustard
150ml / 5 fl oz double cream
175g / 6 oz oyster mushrooms
175g / 6 oz Red Velvet Beetroots sliced
Roasted Chestnuts

Method:

Pre-heat the oven to Gas 6, 200c /400f.

Season the steaks with the salt and freshly milled black pepper.
In a heavy -bottomed large frying pan heat the butter and oil on a medium
heat.

Place the steaks into the pan and cook for 2 minutes on either side.
Pour over the port and beef stock and cook for a further minute either
side. Add the mustard coating the tops of the steaks, cooking again for a
further 2 minutes either side. Remove the steaks to a heat proof serving
dish and keep them warm in a hot oven.

Add the cream to the juices left in the pan, blending them thoroughly.
Add the sliced oyster mushrooms and Beets and cook for 3 minutes, taste
to adjust the seasoning.

Place the mushrooms and beets around the steaks with the sauce and
serve with a few roasted chestnuts.

Serves: 6

CHRISTMAS PYE

I could not resist this 18th century recipe which I have converted for BBC Radio Merseyside Christmas time. I am sure this will be the highlight of some Northern tables on Christmas day.
Quite expensive for today's standards but worth every sixpence.

Ingredients:

175g / 6 oz of the following roughly chopped cooked meats:
turkey, goose, chicken and York ham
50g / 2 oz butter
1 large onion, finely chopped
175g / 6 oz button mushrooms
salt
freshly milled black pepper
6 tablespoons brandy
300ml / 10 fl oz turkey stock
1 teaspoon cornflour blended with a tablespoon of port
150ml / 5 fl oz double cream
350g / 12 oz shortcrust pastry
175g / 6 oz sausage meat
4 hard boiled eggs, shelled
1 egg for washing the pastry

Method:

Pre-heat the oven gas mark 5, 190c/375f.

In a large saucepan melt the butter, add the onion and mushrooms, cooking for 4 minutes, add the meats and cook for a further 8 minutes. Season well, add the brandy and turkey stock, simmer for 10 minutes, add the cornflour and double cream and simmer for 2 minutes, remove from the heat and allow to cool.

Roll out the pastry on a lightly floured surface, use 2/3rds to line a 1.5 litre (two and half pint) pie dish.
Place the sausage meat on the bottom, lined with the hard boiled eggs then the cooled meat mixture.
Roll out the remaining pastry and cover the pie, pressing gently to seal all round. Brush the pie with beaten egg and decorate with the pastry trimmings.

Bake in the centre of the oven for 45-50 minutes.

Serve with baby roast potatoes, parsnips and mint peas.

Serves: 8-10

ROAST PORK WITH APPLE AND CINNAMON

Ingredients:

3 lb / 1 piece of pork, boned and rolled
salt
freshly milled black pepper
2 cloves crushed garlic
1 teaspoon paprika
3 fresh sprigs of thyme, soaked in 6 tablespoons of fresh apple juice
6 tablespoons apple puree
1 teaspoon of cinnamon
1 tablespoon of freshly chopped mint
150ml / 5 fl oz pork stock
1 tablespoon of cornflour mixed with a little apple juice

Method:

Pre-heat the oven to Gas 6, 200c/ 400f.

Rub the pork with the salt, pepper, garlic and paprika and cook in the oven for 30 minutes.
Place the rest of the ingredients except the cornflour into a saucepan and bring to the boil then simmer for 15 minutes.
Thicken with the cornflour.
Baste the meat with the thyme and apple puree sauce every 15 minutes for 1 hour.
Remove the pork to a large serving plate, carve and add the juices to the rest of the thyme and apple sauce.
Serve with the sauce, new potatoes and vegetables in season.

Serves: 4- 6

VENISON ROAST

This recipe takes three days to make ... so you can go downtown and do some shopping in between time... it's one of my favourite Christmas treats, it is also spectacular to look at, garnished with fresh fruit and a sauce.

Ingredients:

3kg / 6 lb haunch of venison
1 large onion chopped
2 garlic cloves, crushed
1 bouquet garni
8 black peppercorns
600ml / 20 fl oz red wine
150ml / 5 fl oz olive oil
2 tablespoons flour, seasoned
2 oranges, juice and rind
1 lemon, juice and rind
150ml / 5 fl oz apple juice
6 tablespoons rowan jelly (page 116)
4 tablespoons port blended with 1 tablespoon of cornflour
freshly chopped parsley
3 x 50g / 2 oz different varieties of red berries, hulled and washed thoroughly.

Method:

Pre-heat the oven to gas 3, 170c/325f.

Trim any excess fat from the haunch. Place the onion, garlic, bouquet garni, peppercorns, wine and olive oil in a very large dish. Add the venison and baste with the marinade. Cover the dish completely with foil and place into the fridge for 2 days.
Drain the venison, strain the marinade and place to one side.
Brush the venison in oil and double wrap it in cooking foil and roast in the centre of the oven for 3 hours.
25 minutes per 450g /1 lb approx. Remove the foil half hour before the end of the cooking time, sift over the flour and baste with the juices.
Turn the heat up to Gas 4, 180c/350c for the last 30 minutes.
Place the marinade into a clean saucepan, reduce by half.
Add the juice and rind of the fruits to the apple juice and reduce that by half in the same saucepan. Add the rowan jelly, port and cornflour allow the sauce to simmer and thicken for 8 minutes.
Place the haunch on a large serving dish, take out about four slices, pour the sauce around and garnish with parsley, red berries and serve with rowan jelly.(see page 116)

Serves: 8 - 10

MY YORK HAM GLAZED WITH APRICOT COMPOTE
That's compote...not compost ! A compote is basically a jam !

Ingredients:

2kg / 4 lb York ham
1 onion stuck with 6 cloves
1 bay leaf
8 peppercorns
300ml / 10 fl oz sweet white wine
50g / 2 oz soft brown sugar
175ml / 6 fl oz crushed/ pureed apricots and juice
2 tablespoon clear honey, warmed
275g / 10 oz apricots sliced

Method:

Pre-heat the oven to Gas 6, 200c/400f.

Soak the ham in sufficient cold water to cover for 4 hours then discard the water.
Put the ham into a large saucepan with the onion, bay leaf, peppercorns and the white wine in the pan, add just sufficient cold water to cover.
Bring to the boil, cover the pan and simmer gently for 2 hours.
Place the brown sugar, apricot puree and juice with the warmed honey into a bowl and mix together.
Drain the ham.
Remove the skin from the ham, scoring the fat into a diamond pattern across the face of the ham. Place the ham into a baking tray, completely smother with the apricot compote mixture.
Bake in the centre of the oven for 1 hour basting every 15 minutes.

Place the York ham onto a serving dish, garnish with sliced apricots and the juices from the roasting tin.

Serves: 8 - 10

RICH PLUM PUDDING

I don't think Christmas is Christmas without Plum pudding... If it's good enough for Snelly its good enough for me.

Ingredients:

25g / 1 oz butter
100g / 4 oz cooking apple, diced
200g / 7 oz dried figs, chopped
100g / 4 oz currants
100g / 4 oz sultanas
225g / 8 oz raisins
200g / 7 oz blanched almonds, chopped
25g / 1 oz hazelnuts, chopped
100g / 4 oz Brazil nuts, chopped
175g / 6 oz stale white breadcrumbs
1 teaspoon mixed spice
100g / 4 oz soft brown sugar
100g / 4 oz cut mixed peel
1 lemon, juice and rind
100g / 4 oz softened butter
100g / 4 oz clear honey, warmed
3 eggs beaten with 2 tablespoons dark rum
3 tablespoons Brandy

Method:

Grease 2 large pudding basins, 750ml / 1.25 pint
Prepare a double steamer or 2 large saucepans to hold the pudding basins, minimum of three quarters full with water.
Put all the fruit with the dried fruits, nuts, breadcrumbs, spice, sugar, peel, lemon juice and rind into a large mixing bowl.
Into a saucepan melt the butter and honey together on a very low heat , allow to cool slightly and gently beat in the eggs and rum.
Pour the liquid over the dried ingredients, stirring thoroughly. Give a final stir adding the brandy.
Spoon the mixture into the greased basins, cover with greased greaseproof paper and secure with string.
Place the basins into the steamers or pans, slowly bring the water to the boil, cover and lower the heat and simmer for 3 hours, topping up with hot water when required.
Allow the Plum pudding to settle for at least 4 hours, then steam again for a further hour before serving.
Put 3 tablespoons of brandy in a metal soup ladle and heat over a low flame, ignite and pour over the pudding when serving, garnished with a sprig of holly.

Serves: 8 - 10

APPLE PIE WITH STILTON CHEESE & PORT

Up North we like to see real apple in our apple pie, not a little pip that's covered in pastry. When eating apple pie it must be just warm, not hot, and served with generous chunks of Stilton or even Lancashire cheese and a glass of Vintage port if it's Christmas,.... but none of your namby, pamby custard .

Ingredients:

900g / 2 lb cooking apples, peeled, cored and thickly sliced
150g / 5 oz soft brown sugar
1 teaspoon freshly grated nutmeg
1 teaspoon crushed cloves
milk to brush the pastry
1 tablespoon caster sugar
450g / 1 lb Wensleydale cheese
100g / 4 oz white and black seedless grapes
50g / 2 oz celery, cleaned and trimmed
50g / 2 oz radish, trimmed

SHORTCRUST PASTRY
350g / 12 oz plain flour
pinch of salt
75g / 3 oz butter
75g / 3 oz lard

To make the pastry, sift the flour and salt into a large bowl, rub in the fats until they resemble fine breadcrumbs. Add just enough cold water to make a stiff dough (4-6 tablespoons).
Knead the pastry for 3 minutes, then roll out the pastry on a lightly floured surface, using 2/3rd to line a 900ml / one and half pint pie dish.

Method:

Pre-heat the oven gas 6, 200c/400f.

Put half the apples into the dish, sprinkle with half the sugar, nutmeg and cloves, top with the rest of the apples, nutmeg and cloves and sugar.
Cover with the remaining pastry, sealing the edges. Brush the pastry with a little milk and dredge with the caster sugar.
Bake in the centre of the oven for 20 minutes, then lower the heat to Gas 4, 180c/350f and bake for a further 15 minutes.
Serve warm, sliced with cheese, garnished with grapes, celery and radish.
And a special Christmas treat of Vintage Port.

Serves: 8

CLIVE'S CHRISTMAS BREAD AND BUTTER PUDDING

Every Christmas is the same, there is always lots of bread left over and jars of mincemeat, bottles and bottles of milk with butter coming out of our ears. So what do we do with it all ?....... Make a Christmas Bread & Butter Pudding. Clive Garner, who presents 'Music and Memories' on Radio Merseyside came up with this one.

Ingredients:

25g / 1 oz butter
12 slices of bread and butter
50g / 2 oz sultanas
400g / 14 oz or 1 jar of mincemeat, warmed
1 teaspoon freshly ground nutmeg
600ml / 20 fl oz milk
3 eggs
50g / 2 oz soft brown sugar
grated nutmeg
brown sugar

Method:

Pre-heat the oven gas 4, 180c /350f.
Grease a large baking dish (2 litre) with 25g / 1 oz butter. Cut the bread into triangles and arrange in alternative layers, buttered side up sprinkled with sultanas, spreading over the mincemeat and grated nutmeg, finishing with a top layer of bread in a neat pattern.
Heat the milk in a saucepan, do not let it boil. Beat the eggs in a bowl with the sugar, whisk in the hot milk. Strain the custard mixture over the bread, finish with a little more grated nutmeg and a little more brown sugar.
Leave the dish to stand for 45 minutes. Bake in the centre of the oven for 35-40 minutes until the custard is set.

Serves: 8

MERRY CHRISTMAS CAKE

The only way to get a kiss under the mistletoe from me is to praise me about my very rich Christmas cake... I should have bin a chef !

Ingredients:

225g / 8 oz butter
225g / 8 oz caster sugar
drops of gravy browning
225g / 8 oz plain flour, sifted with ½ teaspoon baking powder
pinch of salt
1 teaspoon mixed spice
6 eggs, whisked
450g / 1 lb currants
225g /8 oz raisins
100g / 4 oz chopped glace cherries
50g / 2 oz chopped peel
100g / 4 oz blanched, chopped almonds
4 tablespoons of rum

Method:

Pre-heat the oven to gas 3, 170c/325f.

Line a 10 inch cake tin with greaseproof paper.
Place the butter and sugar into a very large bowl and stir until completely blended, add a few drops of gravy browning.
Sift the flour with the baking powder, salt and mixed spice. Add the flour and then the egg mixture alternatively, very carefully until both ingredients are used up.
Add the rest of the ingredients and stir until everything is completely blended.
Let the mixture settle for 1 hour and give it a final stirring.
Put the mixture into the cake tin, and cover top with a piece of greaseproof paper.
Bake in the centre of the oven for 45 minutes.
Lower the heat to Gas 1, 140c/275f for 4 hours.
Remove the cake and allow the cake to cool completely before you remove it from the tin.
Remove the paper. Turn the cake over and sprinkle the bottom with 4 tablespoons of brandy. Double wrap the cake in greaseproof paper, then in cooking foil. Place the cake into a large biscuit tin and store in a cool place for at least a week before decorating and icing for Christmas.

Serves: 10 -12

TIS A SCOUSE TRIFLE

No jelly in this trifle. And I assure you that the flavour is far superior to the ready made so-called trifles that are bought in the stores today.

Ingredients:

4 tablespoons strawberry jam
275g / 10 oz stale sponge cake
6 almond macaroons, crushed
150ml / 5 fl oz cream sherry
350ml / 12 fl oz milk
3 eggs
2 tablespoons caster sugar
vanilla essence
150ml / 5 fl oz double cream, whipped

Method:

Spread the jam over the sponge cake and cut into small cubes. Arrange them in a large glass bowl, add the crushed macaroons and pour over the sherry.

Put the milk into a saucepan and bring gently to the boil.
Into another bowl put the eggs and sugar, mixing them well, slowly add the milk and a few drops vanilla essence, whisking briskly.

Strain the mixture into a clean saucepan and gently bring just to boiling point, simmer for 10 minutes on a very low heat until the custard thickens. Slowly pour the custard over the trifle .

Leave the trifle custard for about 25 minutes until it cools.

To prevent a skin forming, wet a piece of greaseproof paper and place it on the top of the custard.
When cold top with the whipped cream.

Serves: 8

SECTION SEVEN

PRESERVES

What is the first thing that springs to the mind when Jam, Pickle and Preserve is mentioned ?
For me it's Yorkshire Relish, Strawberry Jam, Lemon Curd, Rowan Jelly, Piccalilli, Pickled Onions, Pickled Red Velvet Beets, Pickled Eggs and my favourite Red Cabbage .
Always choose firm-ripe fruits, never use over-ripe fruit or the jam will not set. The only other fruit that should be under-ripe are gooseberries, which are plentiful here in the North of England.

When potting preserves make sure the jars are clean, dry and warm. Fill the jars to the brim with the HOT, finished jam or preserve or jelly. And cover with a round of greaseproof paper. Use plastic coated twist tops and seal while the preserves are hot. Label and date each jar and store in a dry, cool and dark area. Most preserves will keep for up to 12 months.

ANGELA SNELL'S HOMEMADE STRAWBERRY JAM

This is especially for Snelly's wife Angela who puts up with a lot!

Fruits do vary in pectin and acid content, but you can now purchase sugar with pectin, which will ensure a perfect setting in jam every time. When using any of the following Jam recipes always use sugar that has pectin in it.
Should you wish, use your favourite fruit to replace Strawberries using the same method.

Ingredients: (Makes 1.4 kg)
1.4 kg / 3 lb Strawberries
1.4 kg / 3 lb Sugar with Pectin
Juice and rind of $\frac{1}{2}$ lemon

Method:
Hull and wash the strawberries and drain them well and cut them into quarters. Place the strawberries in a large bowl in layers with the sugar and pectin, leaving them for 3 hours.
Put them into a large saucepan, add the lemon with rind and stir for 2 minutes until the lemon is blended.
Bring to the boil rapidly for 8 minutes, then simmer for 20 minutes. Then allow the jam to cool for 15 minutes, removing any scum. Stir the strawberries carefully through the jam.
Pot into warm jars, cover, label and date.

This type of jam will keep for up to 6 months.

LANCASHIRE RELISH

One of the oldest preserves in Lancashire History and in the Inn's and restaurants if meat was covered with gravy the Lancastrain became very suspicious, thinking it was yesterday's left-overs warmed and tarted up. So they would ask for Cold beef with a sauceboat of Lancashire Relish.

Ingredients:

600ml / 20 fl oz malt vinegar
100g / 4 oz soft brown sugar
1 teaspoon of salt
6 black peppercorns
25g / 1 oz chopped chillies
1 tablespoon black treacle
1 tablespoon Worcestershire sauce
1 tablespoon mushroom ketchup
½ teaspoon freshly grated nutmeg

Method:

Place all the ingredients into a saucepan and bring to the boil, simmer for 10 minutes allow the relish to cool.
Pour into warm clean bottles with Cork or vinegar proof tops.
This relish will keep for about 18 months if stored in a dry, dark place and will mature with age.

GOOSESBERRY & ELDERBERRY JAM

The gooseberries should be just under-ripe and all fruits should be washed thoroughly. You can use practically any summer fruits for this recipe.

Ingredients: (Makes about 8lb jam)
900g / 2 lb gooseberries
900g / 2 lb elderberries
water to cover
2 tablespoons lemon juice
2kg / 4½ lb sugar with pectin

Method:

Wash the gooseberries and elderberries, topping and tailing them. Place in a large saucepan and add enough water to cover the fruit.
Bring the fruit to the boil and simmer for 30 minutes until the fruit is soft. Skim the top of the pan, add the lemon juice and sugar with pectin.
Stir until the sugar and pectin is completely dissolved.
Bring to the boil again, boiling rapidly until setting point is reached about 15 to 18 minutes.
Pot and seal the jam.

TOM SLEMEN'S LEMON CURD

This was served at lunch and tea, not just on bread and butter but also in cakes and my mother's cheesecakes. I dedicate this to the man in black Tom Slemen, who appears on BB's show on Thursdays at 3, terrifies everyone, and then disappears!!

Ingredients: (Makes 900g / 2 lb)

4 large lemons, juice and grated rind
225g / 8 oz butter softened
450g / 1 lb caster sugar
5 large eggs, beaten

Method:

Place the lemon juice and grated rind into a bowl over a saucepan of boiling water or a double saucepan.
Whisk in the softened butter and sugar, whisking gently over a low heat until the mixture is completely dissolved.
Take the pan from the heat and allow it to cool for 30 seconds.
Whisk in the beaten eggs. Return the pan to the heat and cook gently again for 5 to 8 minutes until the curd coats the back of the spoon.
Pot and seal the curd.

ROWAN JELLY

The Rowan berries must be just ripe and the apples sweet and ripe.

Ingredients:

900g / 2 lb Rowan berries
900g / 2 lb Cox's Orange pippin
water to cover
2kg / 4½ lb sugar with pectin

Method:

Remove any stalks from the rowan berries, wash and drain them.
Peel, core and chop the apples.
Place the fruits into a large saucepan, and just cover the fruit with water.
Cook for 15 minutes then strain the fruit and liquid through a fine sieve into another clean saucepan.
Add the sugar and pectin.
Boil rapidly for 15 minutes until the jelly is nearly at setting point, pot and seal in warm jars.

This is excellent with any of the Game recipes in this book.

PICCALILLI

You could walk into 95% of any of the homes on Merseyside in the 1960's
and see a jar of Piccalilli on every dining table.
This was a simple and effective way of using up the end of seasonal
vegetables, today we can get the vegetables all year round.

Ingredients:

900g / 2 lb equal mixture of the following vegetables cut into bite size
pieces:-
small cucumbers or gherkins,
baby onions (peeled)
cauliflower florets
75g / 3 oz cooking salt
600ml / 20 fl oz white vinegar
175g / 6 oz granulated sugar
50g / 2 oz dried English mustard powder
1 teaspoon of turmeric
25g / 1 oz cornflour

Method:
Put the vegetables into a large dish and sprinkle with the salt, cover and
leave it to stand for 24 hours.
Wash and rinse the vegetables. In a separate large saucepan put the
vinegar and heat it gently, add the vegetables.
Mix together all the dried ingredients together and add to the vegetables
and the vinegar, stirring and simmer gently for 15 minutes.
Pot and seal with vinegar proof tops.
Leave for at least 2 months before using.

PICKLED RED VELVET BABY BEETS

You can buy these beetroot ready for pickling from Marks &
Spencer's and Sainsbury stores, they have them under their own brand,
but I can assure you they are Red Velvet Baby beetroots.

Ingredients:

900g / 2 lb Red Velvet Baby Beetroot
600ml /20fl oz Red wine vinegar hot but not boiling
12g / ½ oz salt
1 teaspoon of juniper berries

Method:
Put all the ingredients into a glass bowl and stir.
Pack the beets into jars and top up with the vinegar, seal with vinegar
proof tops and leave them to stand for at least 4 to 6 weeks before using
them.

PICKLED ONIONS
For Clarke with an 'e' at the Shakespeare Hotel in Farnworth.

I make my pickled onions quite sweet and I also use a milder vinegar than spiced or pickling vinegar. I find white wine vinegar less tangy and the use of soft brown sugar mellows the sharpness of the pickles should you wish to try my method.

Ingredients:

900g / 2 lb pickling onions, peeled
600ml /20fl oz spiced or pickling vinegar, hot but not boiling
100g / 4 oz soft brown sugar.
12g / ½ oz salt
1 teaspoon of pink peppercorns

Method:

Put all the ingredients into a glass bowl stir with a wooden spoon until the sugar dissolves.
Pack the pickles into jars and top up with the vinegar, seal with vinegar proof tops and leave them to stand for at least 4 to 6 weeks before using them.
To make a spiced vinegar add, 8 cloves, 12g / ½ oz, pieces of ginger and cinnamon with 8 white peppercorns to 1 litre of malt vinegar. Bottle for 2 months and shake the bottle every week.
Strain and use when required.

RED CABBAGE

Try adding some freshly grated Beetroot to the Red Cabbage for a even nicer flavour. This home-made red cabbage will become the talking point of the table. Choose a really firm cabbage, removing any discoloured leaves, cut the cabbage into quarters and cut out the inner stalk.

Ingredients:

1 red cabbage, washed and shredded
100g / 4 oz cooking salt
50g / 2 oz soft brown sugar
600ml / 20 fl oz white wine vinegar

Method:

Place the shredded cabbage, salt and sugar into layers in a large basin, cover with cling film and leave it to stand for 24 hours.
Rinse the cabbage in cold water, draining it well. Pack the cabbage quite loosely into jars and cover with the white wine vinegar and seal.
Let the red cabbage stand for at least 7 days before using and use the red cabbage within 3 months or it will lose its crispness.
P.S. Tastes great with Scouse - (see page 25)

PICKLED EGGS

I once saw a Chinese pickled egg sold at an auction for £1,000...the person who bought it proceeded to eat it there and then, no bread no cheese... nothing.... some people have no etiquette !

The eggs should be boiled for 10 minutes, stirring them after the first 3 minutes to centralise the yolks. Then plunge them into cold water for 12 minutes.

Ingredients:

12 fresh eggs, hard boiled and shelled
600ml / 20 fl oz white wine vinegar
3 blades of mace

Method:

Pack the eggs into glass jars, cover with the vinegar adding a blade of mace to each jar.
Seal and leave for 1 month before using.

BEETROOT & RHUBARB CHUTNEY

Ingredients:

450g / 1 lb diced red Velvet Beetroot
450g / 1 lb rhubarb (red end) , washed and chopped
2 onions, chopped
3 tablespoons sultanas
2 tablespoons soft brown sugar
pinch of cayenne pepper
1 teaspoon salt
1 tablespoon mild curry paste
2 tablespoons of port
150ml / 5 fl oz white wine vinegar

Method:

Put all the ingredients except the beetroot into a large saucepan, bring to the boil and simmer slowly for 5 minutes, stirring all the time.
Boil rapidly for a further 5 minutes until the rhubarb is fully cooked.
Add the Beetroot and blend.
Put into warm jars. Let it stand for 7 days before using.

RASPBERRY VINEGAR

Thanks to Paddy from Kenny for coming up with this one!
Quite amazing over fish and chips

Ingredients:

900g / 2 lb fresh raspberries
2 litre white wine vinegar
900g / 2 lb granulated sugar

Method:

Put the hulled raspberries into a large clean glass bowl.
Pour over enough vinegar to cover the raspberries.

Cover and leave them to stand for 4 days, stirring every day.

Strain the liquid not the raspberries through a non-metallic sieve, being
very careful not to crush the raspberries through the sieve, as this will
make the vinegar cloudy.

Pour the juice into a saucepan add the sugar, bring the juice to the boil
and then simmer for 20 minutes.

Let the liquid stand until it is completely cold and then bottle, using cork
or plastic tops.

Seal and let it stand for at least 4 days before use.
You can use this same method and recipe with any soft fruit berries.

That's it for this book ... happy cooking !

SOME OF TOM'S FAVOURITE FOOD SUPPLIERS

The secret of good cooking is first to have a very passionate love affair with it. Find the finest ingredients and treat them like you would a new born baby, with love and affection. You will all have your own favourite shops on Merseyside and some are listed here, but for those of you a little further afield, here are some places that you can trust. Remember, the most important ingredients are patience, time and the enthusiasm and love of food to bring to life. T.B

Brian Olverson. M.D.
Norman Olverson Ltd
Quality Growers & Packers of Salads & Vegetables
Red Velvet Beetroot
Kershaws Farm Scarisbrick
Ormskirk Lancashire L40 8HN
Telephone 01704 840392

Leading suppliers of cooked beetroot to Sainsbury's, Marks & Spencer and soon to be seen in supermarkets across the UK.

Oliver Kay
Rediveg
Suppliers of Quality Fresh Fruit & Vegetables
Cochrane Street
Bolton BL3 6BL
01204 385463

DC Scott & Sons Ormskirk
Peter Scott
25-27 Church Street
Ormskirk,
Lancashire L39 3AG
01695 572104
Fax 01695 572104

Catherine Smith and Jennifer Lambert
North West Fine Foods
Agriculture House
1 Moss Lane View
Skelmersdale
Lancashire WN8 9TL
01695 554918
Fax 01695 554901

PORT OF LANCASTER SMOKED SALMON Co.
The West Quay, Glasson Dock, Nr. Lancaster, Lancs. LA2 0DB
Tel : 01524 751493
Fax: 01524 752168

A family firm producing a superior grade smoked Scottish salmon, and well known for smoked hams, bacon, cheese, trout, duck breast, chicken and game.

SOUTHPORT POTTED SHRIMPS
66 Station Road, Banks Village, Nr Southport, Lancs, PR98BB
Contact: James Peet
Tel: 01704 229266

FLAVOURFRESH SALADS
Aldergrove Centre, Marsh Road, Banks, Southport, PR9 8DX
Tel: 01704 232223
Fax: 01704 212505
Contact: Ray Plummer
High quality tomatoes, unbeatable in quality, flavour and eating experience.

DEW-LAY
Garstang, Preston, Lancashire, PR3 OPR
Tel: 01995 602 335
Fax: 01995 601 997

Award winning producers of the finest Lancashire cheeses since 1957.

FARM PRODUCE MARKETING LTD.
Harvest House, Newton Lane, Tattenhall, Chester, CH3 9HE
Tel : 01829 771125
Fax: 01829 771601
Producers of "Orchard Maid" luxury frozen yoghurt and Fresh Milk from Cheshire".

RAVENS OAK DAIRY
Burland Farm, Wrexham Road, Burland, Nantwich Cheshire, CW5 8ND
Tel: 01270 524624
Fax: 01270 524724
Hand-made soft and fresh cheeses from Michael and Sandra Allwood.

BOWLAND WILD BOAR Ltd.
Lower Greystoneley, Leagram, Chipping, Preston, Lancashire, PR3 2QT
Tel/Fax : 01995 61554
Wild Boar whole carcass sides, steaks, burgers, sausages and bacon.

CHESHIRE SMOKEHOUSE LTD
The Cheshire Smokehouse, Vost Farm, Morley Green, Wilmslow, Cheshire, SK9 5NU
Tel : 01625 548499
Fax:01625 848606
Dry-cured bacon & hams, smoked fish, charcuterie products and award-winning hams.

HOLLY TREE FARM SHOP
Chester Road, Tabley, Knutsford, Cheshire, WA16 0EU
Contact: Karol Bailey
Tel : 01565 651835
Fax: 01565 632174
Tasty home-produced geese, ducks, turkey, lamb, beef and pork - all traditionally reared and matured the old fashioned way. Over 30 unusual varieties of handmade sausages, pâtés, stuffings,etc.

JOHNSON & SWARBRICK
Swainson House Farm, Goosnargh Lane, Goosnargh, Lancashire, PR3 2JU
Tel: 01772 865251
Without doubt the finest ducklings in the North West.

MORPRO LIMITED (OAKWELL BRAND)
Holt Lane, Netherley Industrial Estate, Netherley, Liverpool, L27 2YB
Tel: 0151 487 3110/3220
Fax: 0151 487 7437
Family run business producing award winning black puddings using the finest ingredients.

TATTON PARK
Tatton Park, Knutsford, Cheshire, WA16 6QN
Tel : 01625 534400
Fax: 01625 534403
Tatton Park produce prime venison, available as frozen packs (steaks, joints or hand diced).

WORRAL HOUSE FARM
Flatman's Lane, Down Holland, (Gt.Altcar), Nr. Ormskirk, L39, 7HW
Tel 0151 527 1210
Contact Lisa & Simon Edwards.
Finest Organic Pork.

HARRY OGILVIE - FAMILY BUTCHERS
111 Oxton Road
Birkenhead
CH41 2TN
Tel: 0151 652 5321

THETIS - The Admiralty Regrets –The Disaster in Liverpool Bay
by C.Warren & J.Benson

The definitive minute by minute account of this terrible tragedy in 1939 when 99 men lost their lives as HM Submarine *Thetis* undertook her first and only dive. With new photographs and documents as well as a new foreword by a survivors son Derek Arnold, and a new postscript by maritime historian David Roberts. Why didn't anyone cut open the submarine? Why was there no urgency in the Admiralty's rescue system? Did the Admiralty really regret?

ISBN 0 9521020 8 0   £9.50 + £1.50 p&p

HMS THETIS – Secrets and Scandal – aftermath of a disaster.
by David Roberts

The sinking of *Thetis* cost 99 men their lives and is still today the worst submarine disaster in British History. This new book contains interviews with relatives of victims; sons, daughters, brothers, sisters and those very rare ladies, living widows. Also here are never before seen documents from the time; Offers of outside help, Secret Navy reports and even descriptions of bodies for identification. Why did the Official Inquiry blame nobody, explaining it away as 'an unfortunate sequence of events'? Why did the civil action on behalf of the widow's fail? Did the Admiralty cover it up? How much did Churchill know?

How were those left behind treated? A huge publicly subscribed disaster fund was collected for the relatives. How was this managed and distributed? Who got what and why? What ever happened to the money that was left?

'a book that shocks…tells the hidden story of those left behind'   - Sea Breezes.

ISBN 0 9521020 0 5   £8.99 + £1.50 p&p

LUSITANIA
by Colin Simpson - updated Merseyside Edition

THE definitive work on the real story surrounding this still mysterious ship.

On the 7th of May 1915 the Cunard vessel Lusitania was torpedoed by a German submarine off the Old Head of Kinsale on the south west coast of Ireland resulting in the loss of the vessel itself and 1,201 men, women and children. It also ultimately resulted in the United States entry to the First World War. More than eighty five years on the story of the *Lusitania* continues to be shrouded in mystery and suspicion. What was her real cargo? Why wasn't she protected? Why did she sink so quickly? Containing rare photographs from Germany and elsewhere; it is a truly intriguing and fascinating tale.

ISBN 0 9521020 6 4   £9.50 + £1.50 p&p

CAMMELL LAIRD - the golden years
by David Roberts. Foreword by Frank Field MP

Looks back at the world famous shipyard's history with particular focus upon the 1960s and 70s when Lairds were engaged in the building of Polaris Nuclear submarines. A unique look at the history of this yard that contains many photographs and references.

'Captures life in the prosperous years of the historic Birkenhead shipyard'- Liverpool Echo
'Puts into perspective…the strikes…the Polaris contract…and those who worked at the yard'- Sea Breezes

ISBN 09521020 2 1   £5.99 + £0.80 p&p

LIFE AT LAIRDS - Memories of working shipyard men
by David Roberts

When Cammell Lairds has gone and we are a generation or two down the line who will answer the questions 'What did they do there?' 'What was it like?' This book answers the questions. - Sea Breezes

A Piece of Social History – Liverpool Echo

Life at Lairds is a book of more than 120 pages about what life was like for the thousands of ordinary people that worked in the world famous Birkenhead shipyard. Contains many rare photographs of Lairds, its' ships and its' surroundings.

ISBN 0 9521020 1 3   £6.99 + £1.50 p&p

Faster Than the Wind - A History Guide to the Liverpool to Holyhead Telegraph.
by Frank Large

Take a journey along the one of most spectacular coastlines in Britain, the beautiful hills and countryside of North Wales and Wirral. On a clear day it is possible to see just how signals were sent along the coast to and from Liverpool. This book contains full details of the intriguing and little known sites of the substantial remains of the Liverpool to Holyhead Telegraph Stations. A second journey can then be taken into the fascinating workings of such a telegraph and those people involved in creating and using the signalling system and what life was really like living and working at the telegraph stations more than 100 years ago.

ISBN 09521020 9 9   £8.95 + £1.50 p&p

Iron Clipper – 'Tayleur' – the White Star Line's 'First Titanic'
by H.F. Starkey

'Iron Clipper' is subtitled 'The First Titanic' for it tells the story of the first White Star liner to be lost on her maiden voyage. Built on the Upper Mersey at Warrington, the *'Tayleur'* tragedy of 1854 and the *'Titanic'* catastrophe of 1912 are disasters which have so much in common that the many coincidences make this factual book appear to be a work which is stranger than fiction.

ISBN 1 902964 00 4   £7.50+ £1.40 p&p

Schooner Port - Two Centuries of Upper Mersey Sail
by H.F. Starkey

Schooner Port tells the story of the part Runcorn and navigation of the upper Mersey played in the Industrial Revolution and of the contribution of merchants, the shipbuilders, and the crews in making Britain 'The Workshop of the World'. Also recounted is something of the courage and tragedy, which was the lot of many flatmen and seamen who helped build British industry on the strength of the shipping fleet.

'Recognised as the only authoritative work on this particular subject '- Sea Breezes

'Packed with hard facts and illustrated with some rare old photographs, this rare book should command a wide readership'. - Liverpool Echo

ISBN 0 9521020 5 6   £8.95 + £1.50 p&p

THE GOLDEN WRECK - THE TRAGEDY OF THE ROYAL CHARTER
by ALEXANDER MCKEE

The effects great of the great hurricane of October 1859 were to shock the nation. 133 ships were sunk, 90 were badly damaged and almost 800 people lost their lives.

More than half of those that perished were on one ship - The *Royal Charter*, when she was lost off Anglesey on her way home to Liverpool from the Australian Goldfields.

News of the wreck soon spread and the *Royal Charter's* other cargo, gold, became the focus of people's attention. Was all of it ever recovered? If not where did it go? The *Royal Charter's* gold still has the power to attract the adventurous and this book also explores attempts at salvage and treasure hunting more than 140 years on. £9.50 & 1.50 p&p ISBN 1 902964 0 20

JUST NUISANCE AB - His full story
by Terence Sisson

The amazing but true story of the only dog that was officially enlisted into British Royal Navy, a Great Dane whose name was Nuisance, his official rank and name was AB Just Nuisance.

Famed for his preference for the company of navy ratings (he wasn't too keen on Officers) in and around the famous World War II naval base of Simonstown, South Africa, Nuisance helped many a sailor rejoin his ship after a night on the town.

Today his own statue overlooking the bay off the Cape of Good Hope commemorates AB Just Nuisance. £7.50 & £1.20 p&p

FORGOTTEN EMPRESS
-The tragedy of the Empress of Ireland
by David Zeni

This book tells the fascinating story of 'Liverpool's Lost Empress', the Canadian Pacific Passenger liner *RMS Empress of Ireland*. On her way home to Liverpool from Canada, she was sunk in a collision on the St. Lawrence River.

Two years after the *Titanic*, it was, in terms of passenger fatalities, an ever greater tragedy.

These two ships, along with the *Lusitania*, form a triumvirate of maritime disasters, all within a three year period, that sent shock waves around the world.

Yet whilst *Titanic* and *Lusitania* seem to be almost household names, the disaster that befell the *Empress of Ireland* has until now always been shrouded in the cloak of history, as impenetrable as the fog that brought about her total loss, along with 1,012 lives, on 29th May 1914.

With a chilling connection to the 'Crippen Murders' and containing never-before-published material including comprehensive crew and passenger lists, Forgotten Empress grips the reader in such a way it is hard to put aside... a thoroughly excellent book.

'...dubbed 'The 'Forgotten Empress'...the second in a shocking trio of tragedies at sea...sandwiched in between the disasters of the Titanic and the Lusitania, ...it was a sudden death... that sent Liverpool into mourning...'

Liverpool Echo

'Zeni brings a fresh, moment by moment urgency to this real life tragic drama'

Winnipeg Free Press

£12.50 inc p&p ISBN 1 902964 15 2

UNION - CASTLE -The Forgotten Navy- by Peter Abbott

The Union - Castle Shipping Company was rightly famed for the Mailships of the line such as the Pendennis Castle and the Windsor Castle but there is much more to Union-Castle than just these well-known liners.

'Union-Castle - the Forgotten Navy' features the Intermediate liners, The Royal East Africa Service, Round Africa vessels, coasters, general cargo ships and reefers. It also covers the Zulu War, Boer War, World War I and World War II.

Using records from company archives, contemporary South African newspapers, the author's own and others private collections of Union-Castle ephemera, this new book about 'the Forgotten Navy' brings the reader a significant amount of hitherto little known material about the ships, the people and the Union-Castle Company.

£10.00 inc p&p ISBN 1 902964 21 7

LUSITANIA AND BEYOND
- THE STORY OF CAPTAIN WILLIAM THOMAS TURNER

by Mitch Peeke & Kevin Walsh- Johnson. Illustrated by John Gray

There are many accounts of the great maritime disasters, but very few portraits of the people at the centre of these vast, tragic events. William Thomas Turner was captain of the RMS *Lusitania* when the giant liner was sunk by a German submarine attack in May 1915, with the loss of more than 1,200 passengers and crew. Turner survived, and this is his story.

A Merseyside man, he came from Victorian seafaring stock and his sole ambition was always to go to sea. Turner became the outstanding seaman of his time, who had learned his craft the hard way- by experience.

The loss of the *Lusitania*, bound for Liverpool from New York, shattered his world and over the years he has been accused of treachery, stubbornness, ignorance and much worse. This book gives the true, remarkable story of Captain William Thomas Turner, the last Master of the doomed *Lusitania*. ISBN 0 902964 14 4   £7.99 + £1.25 p&p

'...the Admiralty made 'thoroughly discreditable attempts to blame Turner for the loss'
'...clears Captain Turner's name once and for all'...   Liverpool Echo

ALL at SEA
- Memories of Maritime Merseyside

Compiled by Ev Draper. Foreword by Radio Merseyside's Linda McDermott
Introduction by David Roberts - Maritime Historian

A new book in conjunction with BBC Radio Merseyside's programme of the same name brings the voices of Merseyside seafarers and their lives to the printed page. Here are the stories of brave men, now pensioners, who survived horrendous incidents in the last two wars; stories of luxury liners, from Captains to cabin crew, of young lads forging their identity cards to get away to sea, and of their first eye-opening voyages.

ALL at SEA brings back the sounds and the smells of the docks, which remain vivid in so many people's minds, of busy tugs up and down the river, of men lost at sea; of women serving their country in different ways, and of those who provided guiding lights home. But through all the stories, there's one shining thread, the pride of Merseysiders in their seagoing traditions.

If you want real stories of the sea, told from the heart, by real people about real times and places, then this is a book for you. ISBN 1 902964 12 8   £5.99 + £1.25 p&p

FROM BATTLEFIELD TO BLIGHTY

The History of Frodsham Military Hospital 1915-1919 by Arthur R Smith

The horrors of the first 'Great War' are well known, but the stories of those sent back from the 'Battlefield to Blighty' tend to be overlooked. This is the little known story of one of the largest auxiliary military hospitals in the country that was established at Frodsham in Cheshire during the First World War.

Over the period of the hostilities more than 3,000 patients were cared for at Frodsham Auxiliary Military Hospital and using a recently discovered set of contemporary photographs, *'From Battlefield to Blighty'* tells the stories of the doctors, the nurses, the patients and the local people who were involved in the Auxiliary Military Hospital at Frodsham. ISBN 1 902964 16 0   £7.99 +1.50 p&p

A Welcome in the Hillsides?

- The Merseyside & North Wales Experience of Evacuation 1939-1945

by Jill Wallis

A book that is both informative and moving, with the stories of the thousands of children who left the dangers of Merseyside for the safety of North Wales during World War II.

ISBN 1 902964 13 6   £9.95 + £1.80 p&p

VIDEOS

Cammell Laird - Old Ships and Hardships - the story of a shipyard.

After an extensive search for moving footage of this world famous shipyard at work a video of the history of this shipyard has at last been compiled. How Cammell Laird served the nation through two World Wars, building world famous vessels like the *Rodney, Hood, Mauritania, Ark Royal, Windsor Castle* and many more, up to the tragic day in 1993 when Lairds was shut down.

The story of the yard is also told through the voices of the men who worked at Lairds; Welders, cranedrivers, electricians and plumbers, they tell of the hardships of building ships in all weathers and the lighter moments that came from some of the 'characters' of the yard. £14.99 including post and packaging in UK.

'All in a Day's work.' Volumes I & II

– a look at working lives on the River Mersey.

Just when you might have thought that the River Mersey was dead and buried the biggest surprise of all comes along. There is life in the old dog yet! The River Mersey is alive and well. Liverpool, Birkenhead, Tranmere, Eastham and Runcorn are still places that enjoy marine traffic and employ people working on the river. There are interviews with River Pilots, shipbuilders, shiprepairers, tugmen and dredgermen that show that the age-old crafts and seamanship itself are still as strong as they ever were. There is also archive footage of working life on the river.

Features Rock Boats, Mersey Ferries, the Bunker boats & crews on the Mersey, the Vessel Tracking System for river traffic, new vessels on the river, lockmasters and much more.

£14.99 including post and packaging in UK.

All videos are available in international formats for £17.99 + P&P £3.50.

Please state country/ format required.